Family Education in Mental Illness

'Family Education in Mental Illness,

AGNES B. HATFIELD

THE GUILFORD PRESS
New York   London

© 1990 The Guilford Press
A Division of Guilford Publications, Inc.
72 Spring Street, New York, NY 10012

Printed in the United States of America

This book is printed on acid-free paper.

Last digit is print number: 9 8 7 6 5 4 3 2 1

Library of Congress Cataloging-in-Publication Data

Hatfield, Agnes B.
    Family education in mental illness / Agnes B. Hatfield.
      p. cm.
    Includes bibliographical references.
    ISBN 0-89862-427-4.—ISBN 0-89862-520-3 (pbk.)
    1. Mentally ill—Family relationships. 2. Adjustment
(Psychology)—Study and teaching. I. Title.
    [DNLM: 1. Adaptation, Psychological. 2. Family. 3. Mental
Disorders—psychology. 4. Social Adjustment. WM 100 H362f]
RC455.4.F3H38 1990
362.2′042—dc20
DNLM/DLC
for Library of Congress   89-71487
                                        CIP

ACKNOWLEDGMENTS

I would like to take this opportunity to acknowledge the historical role played by Clara Claiborne Park in challenging mental health professionals to develop better ways to provide practical help to families who are coping with mental illness in a member. Many professionals now working with families are not aware of Clara Park and Leon Shapiro's pioneering work *You Are Not Alone*, published in 1976, which set a new direction in attitudes toward these families and in ways of working with them. I remember with warmth and gratitude my visit to the Park home in Williamstown, Massachusetts, in 1976, and the encouragement that I received for pursuing the concern of families and mental illness.

I am grateful to Stan Weinstein, Ph.D., and Henry Harbin, M.D., of the Maryland Mental Hygiene Administration for providing me with the opportunity in 1981 to begin developing a statewide educational program for families with mentally ill relatives. Most of my ideas for helping families have come from the Family Education Program of Maryland, as the project came to be called. Evelyn McElroy, Ph.D., R.N., and Elizabeth Farrell, L.C.S.W., later joined me as consultants and helped shape my ideas and the nature of the program.

Of course I learned the most from the several hundred families with whom we have had contact. These families have kept us from being overconfident about how much we know, and they have provided us with the continuous challenge to struggle for more and better answers to their interminable problems. It is their courage and persistence in coping with one of life's most devastating problems that fuels our desire to continue working.

This book provides the curriculum content and the methodology for an educational approach to helping families with a mentally ill relative. The material in this book has grown out of the author's 14 years of experience studying these families, getting to know them personally, assessing their experiences and their needs, and devising educational programs to meet these needs. The past decade has witnessed a rapid growth in interest in educational approaches to family problems, but there have been no comprehensive guidelines available for the newly emerging family educators. We hope that this book will begin to fill some of that void.

In Section I of this book, we identify the basic substructure on which we believe all educational programs should be based: an understanding of the current cultural context for providing services to the mentally ill (see Chapter 1) and an empathic understanding of the people whom we purport to be helping (see Chapters 2 and 3). These understandings lead us to conclude in Chapter 4 that support and education are probably the most appropriate ways for us to work with families. These concepts are developed in this chapter along with the related concepts of family consultation and psychoeducation.

In Section II, we provide a relevant knowledge base from which family educators can select curriculum content for their educational programs. This content is based on what we have learned from families as to their perception of their needs. Usually, they want to understand the mental illness of their relative from both the scientific and the personal perspective. We provide these understandings in Chapters 5 and 6. Families also want to know the relevant treatments for mental illness and the ways that they can support these treatments (see Chapter 7), and they want to know a range of practical coping strategies, which we provide in Chapters 8, 9, and 10.

In Section III, we shift from curriculum or the "what" of education to methodology or the "how" of teaching. In Chapter 11, we establish basic principles of adult learning and provide guide-lines for effective and efficient learning. Emphasis is on didactic teaching and the use of instructional materials. The next chapter (see Chapter 12) we devote to the development of generic problem-solving skills that enhance the capacity of families to become more independent in developing coping strategies. Believing that effective educational programs for families necessarily contain a good measure of personal support, we develop an understanding of the meaning and expression of supportive relationships in Chapter 13.

Chapter 14 concludes our work by pointing to some of the issues that must be considered in family education and by remind-ing our readers to avoid thinking of current family educational approaches as finished products or as models that can be cloned. We point to the pitfalls of insisting upon ownership of programs or creating new kinds of dogma that can only result in irrelevance and stagnation. We encourage constant evolution and renewal of the ideas we have presented here. We owe this much to the fami-lies that we purport to help.

CONTENTS

I

The Family and Mental Illness

CHAPTER 1

The Social Context

Attention to the role of families in the support and care of their mentally ill relatives, once nonexistent, has now achieved a central place in planning for community care of the mentally ill. As a consequence, a range of new approaches to helping families is emerging and with it new issues and controversies. What is the most effective and economical way to meet the needs of those burdened with the problems that accompany mental illness? While there is no definitive answer to that question, there is research and literature on needs of families that can be helpful, and there are programs that have been tried and to some degree evaluated. Local conditions and the range and appropriateness of services to clients must be considered for they tend to dictate the number of options families have. Financial considerations and interested and available staff, of course, also play a part. These and other issues will be addressed later.

We would like to introduce the topic of helping families within a wider context, for we believe that we cannot address their problems in isolation from the particular context in which they arise. Programs of social service fail when they ignore the social framework in which they are a part. The social, political, and historical context in which a problem is embedded too often goes unexamined (Hersch, 1972; Levine, 1981; Sarason, 1981). It is one thing to identify the most exemplary program, but it is quite another thing to anticipate correctly its potential for success in a particular time and place. The more clearly we can identify the relevant political and social factors, the more likely programs can be brought to fruition. So what are some of the current factors that influence the social context in which programs for families are created? We suggest that the following are primary: (1) new definitions of men-

tal illness; (2) changing attitudes toward parents; (3) social decisions regarding responsibility for care of the mentally ill; (4) growth
of the consumer movement; and (5) problems with cost of care.

New Definitions of Mental Illness

Although understanding of mental illness is far from complete,
much has been learned in the past couple of decades that has
changed our definition of mental illness in a very profound way.
Nowhere is there greater change than in the way the basic sciences
are contributing to the understanding of mentally disordered patients. One of the fastest growing and most vital areas in biomedi-
cine is the study of the brain and brain dysfunction. Emphasizing
the significance of this research, Judd (1986) states that "it is quite
clear that the developments and discoveries from the biological
sciences will shape, in very basic and fundamental ways, the practice of psychiatry in the future" (p. 13). As psychiatry is influenced,
one would predict, so will be the rest of the disciplines in mental
illness. "The field is growing so fast," notes Sabshin (1986), the
medical director of the American Psychiatric Association, "that it
becomes gratuitous to point it out" (p. 48). Responding to these
changes will be a challenge to all those in mental health disciplines.
      While the intellectual and philosophical roots of psychiatry as
a discipline have always been grounded on biomedical concepts,
the influence of the psychoanalytical point of view in this country
was so great that for many decades inquiry into the nature and
etiology of mental illness was focused away from inquiry about the
brain and its biological processes and toward psychological explanations of disorders. In addition, there was a lack of sophisticated
technology to study brain mechanisms until lately (Judd, 1986;
Sabshin, 1986).
      The psychoanalytic movement carried great intellectual fer-
vor and had considerable impact on American psychiatry. It resulted in a kind of universal theory of human deviance in which all
mental and emotional problems ranged on a continuum from the
minor stresses of everyday living to the severe disturbances of
schizophrenia. Differences were thought to be quantitative rather
than qualitative. In other words, a minor neurosis could become a
major psychosis if it went untreated. Concomitant with this trend
was a tendency to undertreat patients with blatant and severe
disorders. The emphasis was on prevention of mental illness by
treating minor problems and changing social conditions. But the

fact that there is no evidence that these approaches have reduced mental illness has not persuaded its adherents (Judd, 1986; Maxmen, 1985; Sabshin, 1986). This tendency to de-emphasize mental illness is still apparent in the community mental health movement, which has never developed centers for specializing in the serious, long-term mental illnesses.

This blurred definition of mental illness produced severe boundary problems for the field of mental health which in turn led American policy makers and insurance companies to see psychiatry as a bottomless pit. It appeared that psychopathology was everywhere and that there were few social and personal problems that were not grist for ministrations by mental health practitioners. This problem was less prevalent in other countries where mental illness was defined more narrowly (Sabshin, 1986).

Maxmen (1985) believes that psychiatrists have begun to clarify their area of expertise. They no longer claim that there are no limits on their powers to alleviate personal and social problems. They now distinguish between "mental disorders" and "problems of living." Maxmen distinguishes between the two by stating that the mentally ill have *symptoms* such as delusions, hallucinations, mania, and depression. People with "problems of living" do not have symptoms; instead, they are seeking help with *issues* in their daily lives as to how to improve their marriage, get along better with their boss, raise competent children, etc. People with schizophrenia have symptoms; they are ill and need treatment. Their families face many issues such as how to have their relatives comply with treatment, how to support and motivate them, and how to locate and access services. These families do not need treatment. They need education, advice, and support.

Judd (1986) believes that we are now in a period when the existing conceptual framework and available technology make it possible to restructure the discipline. What seems to us to be emerging at this historical juncture is a clear and definite separation into two distinct fields. The first might be called the field of "mental illness," which treats and rehabilitates those with long-term, highly disabling dysfunctions of the brain, most of whom are diagnosed as having schizophrenia or an affective disorder. The other field might be called "mental health," or a similar name, which concerns itself with quite a different matter—the alleviation of stress due to overwhelming situational problems. These distinct fields require significantly different fields of research, professional training, and social policy. Those who serve the mentally ill need a heavy concentration of training in brain biology, in the perceptions and characteristics of those living with severe mental illnesses, and in the latest in treatment and rehabilitation. Eventually there may need to be a credentialing of those who are especially trained to work with the mentally ill. This is a time of rapid advances; it will be a formidable challenge for practitioners to keep up-to-date, and to be ready to make pragmatic applications in the care of patients with brain disorders.

It is interesting to note that at the founding meeting of the National Alliance for the Mentally Ill (NAMI) in 1979, its members did not hesitate to define the organization's focus as "mental illness." The members, made up of families who for the most part lived on an everyday basis with mental disorder, felt that they knew what mental illness was, that it was not "mental health" that they were interested in, and that the name of their organization should carry the words "mental illness." This identification does not lead to any particular problem in communicating with the public nor to confusion in the minds of possible members.

It is fascinating to contemplate the evolution of the emerging definition of mental illness as outlined above in light of a similar development occurring in the field of autism a couple of decades earlier. For a brief historical review, we turn to Schopler and Mesibov (1984). Kanner, they note, first identified autism 40 years previous, and because he did so during the period of psychoanalytic prominence, he considered it to be an emotional disturbance caused by poor parenting, which was amenable to treatment by therapy. As a consequence of empirical research, and the advocacy work of the National Society for Autistic Children (NSAC), the definition of autism changed to that of a developmental disability with consequent better community understanding followed by better social policies, changed attitudes toward parents, and appropriate behavioral training for those with the disorder. Clearly how we define a problem can make a world of difference. NSAC was founded about a decade before NAMI and for similar reasons: They both recognized that the hope for their impaired relative lay with them and they both were fed up with their scapegoat status for a tragedy not of their own making. Since its inception in 1969, NSAC has been influential in changing the definition of autism from "severe emotional disturbance" to that of a developmental disability in the regulations of Public Law 94-142, the Education of All Handicapped Children's Act (see Warren, 1984). By being included in this act, people with autism have had a wide array of resources open to them, and their parents have been given considerable power to influence treatment plans. In 1982 autism was further defined as a neurological disorder when a special section on autism was established in the National Institute of Neurology and Communicative Disorders and Stroke (NINCDS), a part of the National Institutes of Health (NIH) (see Warren, 1984).

In summary, it can be stated that there is a clear trend toward a new conceptualization of mental illness as a disorder of brain malfunction and, as such, the field has begun to separate itself from the situational disorders that many people experience during the course of a lifetime. These latter disorders may be stressful and require help from time to time but few would call them mental illnesses or attribute them to malfunctions of the brain.

Changing Attitudes toward Parents

Attitudinal changes toward parents with a mentally ill offspring have been marked during the past decade. Now parents are seldom seen as causative agents in their child's tragic disorders, rather they are now seen as an essential part of support and care. Although not all practitioners reflect these changes in attitude, a growing number do. The reasons for this dramatic reorientation probably lie in both political considerations and in recent critiques of psychosocial research. The latter will be addressed first.

Just as autism was once attributed to a wide range of destructive family behaviors, so too has mental illness been attributed to craziness-making families. During the dominance of psychoanalytic theory, early family interactions were considered to be sufficient explanation for any and all adult problems and, therefore, schizophrenia. But psychoanalysts, who are not noted for rigorous scientific research, by and large, did not establish any causal relations between family style and adult pathology. Later, it appeared that new directions were being set when interest developed in the whole family as a system and the relationship of that system to later psychosis in a member. However, these family theorists, many of them first trained as psychoanalysts, did not depart that much from their earlier roots, and therefore hypothesized family pathology in the etiology of mental illness.

It is not the purpose of this chapter to review the theory and research of these family experts. This has already been done in a very substantial way by Hirsch and Leff (1975) and more recently by Howells and Guirguis (1985). Howells and Guirguis make very clear the standards that must be met by researchers in order to establish a causal link between parental behavior and schizophrenia in an offspring: definitions of schizophrenia must be clear, subjects must be randomly sampled, safeguards must be used to avoid biased observations, and attention must be given to the criteria that establish a causal link. To say that something causes schizophrenia, one must establish that something preceded the onset of the disease; there must also be consistency in replication, the link must be strong and specific, and findings must be consistent with well-known facts about schizophrenia.

Using these scientific criteria, Howells and Guirguis have examined the work of several family theorists. Murray Bowen (1960) reported marked "emotional divorce" between parents, parental immaturity and inability to make decisions, and maternal over-investment in the patient. These anomalies supposedly take three generations to produce. Lyman Wynne shared a period as a colleague at the NIMH with Bowen. Wynne and his colleagues focused on intrafamilial patterns of communication (Wynne, 1987; Wynne, McDaniel, & Weber, 1987). They reported that families of schizophrenic persons have forms of thinking disorganization similar to those of their disturbed member. Neither of these researchers meet the Howell and Guirguis definition of acceptable research.

Don Jackson and his colleagues at Palo Alto (Bateson, Jackson, Haley, & Weakland, 1956) developed the notion that schizophrenia is not an illness but a mode of communication. They were particularly interested in the double bind as a form of communication which somehow leads to psychosis. Theodore Lidz (1973) and his colleagues at Yale studied a small number of families of schizophrenics and reported that schizophrenic people behave in a peculiar fashion because their parents are peculiar. Howells and Guirguis (1985) see the Yale studies as "purely descriptive and anecdotal, lacking the rigorous methodological techniques that are the only available means of giving credibility to any findings" (p. 186). They criticize all of the family studies for their methodological shortcomings and for their basic assumption that neuroses and psychoses lie along a continuum, from mild to severe. They state that neuroses and schizophrenia are qualitatively different phenomena.

With no solid evidence supporting family causality of mental illness and with strong evidence for organic causes emerging, the basis for family blaming or seeing families in negative and pejorative ways seems less defensible. Indeed a number of newer family therapists have decried the damage done by past theorizing and seek more collaborative relationships with families (Anderson,

Reiss, & Hogarty, 1986; Bernheim & Lehman, 1985; Beels & McFarlane, 1982; Falloon, Boyd, & McGill, 1984). Nevertheless, one cannot be totally sanguine about this transition. In a recent study of language used by a number of newer family therapists (Hatfield, 1986), the author found there was much that was demeaning in the way families were labeled and described. Obviously, attitude change does not occur quickly.

It is quite possible that factors other than new research findings have major influence on the change of professional attitudes. These are the social and political forces that impinge upon service delivery and the empowerment of new social groups to define problems and influence solutions.

A review of the literature in the last 2 or 3 decades reveals little change in attitudes toward families until well into the 1970s. By that time the deinstitutionalization movement was well along and serious efforts were being made to assess the consequences. It was revealed that local communities had made little preparation to reintegrate their mentally ill citizens and that most discharged patients returned to their families to live (Minkoff, 1978). Mental health professionals found themselves in direct contact with families in a new way, and they began to realize how dependent they were on families for the survival of the experiment in community care. It was no longer politically feasible to view families as pathological, noxious, dysfunctional, and in need of treatment when they needed these families to see themselves as competent and strong enough to provide 24-hour daily care. This political need to see families differently plus changes in perception that occur with frequent face-to-face contact were undoubtedly factors that led to more positive attitudes toward families.

Another social development that played a significant role in changing attitudes toward parents was the emergence of a strong consumer advocacy movement, the NAMI. Not surprisingly, members of the organization reacted strongly to what they perceived as blaming, pejorative attitudes, and abuse by mental health professionals. It became apparent that many of these families were behaving very much like other unempowered people in our society— blacks, gays, and women—when they finally got a voice. Families spend a lot of time explaining how having mental illness in the family affects them, how various professional behaviors and attitudes can be either hurtful or helpful, and what kinds of practical help they need in order to cope successfully. Consciousness raising has been going on much like it did in other movements. Parents have become particularly resistant to being defined as "psychotic-level families," "pathogenic," "dysfunctional," "multi-problemed and disorganized," "high EE families," etc. These are negative judgments, that could lead to self-rejection and low esteem if families were persuaded of their truth. All people, families of the mentally ill included, strive for a self-image that is acceptable to them. Gays and women used direct social action against psychiatrists to force them to abandon language and perceptions that were an anathema to them (Hatfield, 1986). Presumably mental health professionals have learned from those experiences, and are now listening to parents of the mentally ill.

The rapidity of growth and the level of activity of the NAMI have empowered a new group to speak for the mentally ill and their families. Prior to the formation of this organization in 1979, there was no strong consumer voice. It is now generally recognized that the development of NAMI is one of the most critical events for the mentally ill in recent years.

Consumer Power

Until the appearance of the NAMI on the mental health scene, there was little input in service planning by consumers. Historically, those who used and/or paid for mental health services and who were most personally affected by the outcome had little to say about their quality and appropriateness. Western traditions in the helping professions led to paternalism. The power of professionals resided in the fact that they defined the problems, determined the solutions, and evaluated the outcomes. This benign authoritarianism bred passive and compliant consumers (Dewar, 1978; McKnight, 1977).

The tendency in our culture has been to depend on the various professions to regulate their own members. But questions have arisen recently as to how vigorous this regulation has been and whether the consumer has been well protected. Consumers of mental health services are beginning to realize that they must take primary responsibility to insure that treatments are safe and efficacious (Hatfield, 1984, 1987b).

Hollander (1980) believes that we are, indeed, in a revolutionary period with regard to mental health care and that this revolution reflects a larger culture-wide ideology that assumes that consumers are capable of being the primary directors of their service needs and that they need not rely on a hierarchy of experts to make decisions for them. The consumer now recognizes that expert opinion is not a part of an apolitical service system, rather it is a part of a particular interest that is not always that of the consumer (McKnight, 1977).

One might wonder why the public has demanded so little accountability from mental health professionals. McKnight explains that those whose profession is that of "doing good" are assumed to be doing only that; in other words, that they have no self-interest or personal motives. Of course, this is not possible as we all have personal needs met by the work we do. Behind the masks of service are their systems, techniques, and technologies. They are businesses in need of markets, economies seeking new growth potential, and professionals in need of an income. These are realities that consumers must recognize if they are to be successful in the marketplace.

With the growth of the consumer movement, families of the mentally ill began to see themselves as "customers" who, as a matter of right and good economics, insisted on knowing the nature of services being offered to them, evidence as to their effectiveness, risks inherent in them, and accurate projections of their cost–benefits. They began to insist that professionals live up to their own statements of ethical principles and be vigorous in policing their own members (Hatfield, 1983). But are mental health professionals paying any attention? Beels (1978) believes that it is politically inevitable that they do so. The politics and economics of psychiatry is such that it cannot ignore consumers.

Families of the mentally ill, like other consumers of goods and services in our society, want the power of informed choice. They want safe, efficacious, cost-effective help. They want increased control over their own lives. Making informed choices in the arena of mental health, however, presents nearly insurmountable difficulties because there is such a confusing diversity of theory and practice. A typical family seeking help in the management of a mentally ill relative may be told over a short period of time that their relative's difficult behavior is due to the parents' marital problems, high expressed emotion (high EE), communication style, under- or overinvolvement with the patient; they may even be told that their relative is misbehaving rather than ill. This diversity and disunity in the professions produces real credibility problems. Families may end up losing confidence in all of mental health.

NAMI is providing education to its members so they can understand the different family theories, how various theorists have seen the relationship of family life to mental illness, what research has shown, and what the implications are for interventions with families. NAMI has recently published a pamphlet entitled *A Consumer Guide to Mental Health Services* (Hatfield, 1985), which advises families as to how to interview prospective doctors and other service personnel—what questions to ask and what judgments to make in order to get a good fit between the user and provider of services.

Often overlooked in the area of consumer power is the role played by people outside of the service system in influencing service utilization. There is evidence that people seeking help in our culture are highly subjected to the influence of nonprofessional advisors—family, friends, neighbors, and other informal sources, called the "lay referral network" by Gottlieb (1976). The influence of lay referral has, no doubt, been greatly enhanced by the NAMI self-help movement in which members advise each other about satisfactory and unsatisfactory services. In addition, NAMI groups offer emotional support, information, and advice that may sometimes serve as an alternative to professionally provided services. Gottlieb calls this a "lay treatment network" and observes that these nonjudgmental treatment modalities may serve as important alternatives for many families.

Empowerment of consumers can be threatening to some mental health professionals. They are not used to being questioned about their theories, their expertise, and their priorities (Lamb & Oliphant, 1978). Other professionals welcome the new development; they are hopeful that consumers can promote improved services and accountability in ways that professional regulation has not been able to achieve. They support new approaches to service in which power and responsibility are shared in genuinely collaborative ways.

Further consumer empowerment will affect programs for families in a very real way. Families will expect to be in on the planning of new programs, and will expect professionals to share with them theories being implemented, assumptions being made, and evidence of efficacy.

Fiscal Restraint

Hard to ignore in the present social context is the preoccupation of social planners with the high cost of medical and mental health services and the need for fiscal restraint. This is a relatively recent preoccupation and one that it is difficult for practitioners to come to terms with. Nevertheless, in planning for help to families, this is a reality that cannot be ignored.

Health-care costs in the United States have been rising at a rapid rate over the past 2 decades. In 1960 less than 5% of the gross national product (GNP) was spent for health care. In 1983, these expenditures represented 10.8% of the GNP (Sharfstein & Beigel, 1985). High-level discussions are going on as well as much rethinking on the part of employers, employees, providers, insurance carriers, and consumers as to how our society can afford to pay for all the health services Americans have come to expect.

Frank and Kamlett (1985) have estimated that direct costs and expenditures for mental health care in 1980, including figures from the mental health sector, the general medical sector, and the human service sector, which incorporates transportation costs and transfer of payments, range between $19.2 and $22 billion per year. Even with this huge expenditure, both consumers and providers are well aware that the seriously mentally ill are vastly underserved. Most providers believe that a great influx of new money is required. A few, such as Torrey and Wolfe (1986), believe that there is little relationship between the excellence of service and dollars spent.

There was a time when medical insurance covered most physical health needs, and to a lesser extent mental health needs, demanded by consumers. But the picture is changing, and among those highly concerned are employers. Once employers found it to their fiscal advantage to offer employees substantial fringe benefits as a part of their earnings. Among the most important fringe benefits was health coverage. Problems began to occur when costs to insurers rose rapidly, which was due to stimulated demand and rising costs for unit of service (Talbott & Dauner, 1985). The consuming public and employers who paid for these costs were becoming cost conscious.

McGuire (1981) notes that the problem is that emotional distress is ubiquitous, that anyone can qualify as needy, and that once treatment commences, it may continue indefinitely. Mechanic (1978) concurs. The knowledge and treatment of mental illnesses remain so uncertain, he says, that it is difficult for policy makers to differentiate between mental illness and the abundant problems and frustrations of everyday life. Insurance carriers want to avoid the quagmire of defining mental illnesses so protect themselves with high coinsurance, deductibles, and cost ceilings.

Gaylin (1985) believes that we are truly entering a new era in health care service. "The pressure for change is so strong," he states, "is so specific in direction, and has reached such critical levels that it is no longer a question of whether it is good or bad; the trend cannot be halted" (p. 158). He believes that innovative programming will move more toward prepaid groups and away from private practice psychotherapy. The insurance issues will probably continue to evolve for some time to come; but even though unsettled, these issues cannot be ignored when planning work with families.

To the extent that private insurance is limited for work with families, we must consider the possibilities in the area of tax-supported institutions and agencies. We know that community mental health centers (CMHCs) are increasingly offering workshops, classes, and therapy to assist families. It is important to recognize, however, that CMHCs are experiencing an uncertainty of their own. CMHCs, once directly subsidized by the federal government, are undergoing major changes in the ways money is being distributed, and the total amount given to them has been reduced. Precisely how these changes will affect the amount and kinds of services is still unknown.

In spite of the unsettled financial picture, however, interest in helping families is on the rise, and new programs are emerging. Those who succeed with these programs will need to find ways to support them in spite of the dollar crunch. Sometimes it is in difficult and unsettled times that truly innovative services are invented.

Responsibility for Care

A primary issue in helping families is what roles they will be playing in the support and care of their disabled relative. This issue, once resolved, will be the most important factor in designing programs for families. We know now that a large proportion of persons with mental illness will need long-term care, some possibly for the rest of their lives. What has never been resolved is who is responsible for this care.

The future may hold a somewhat different balance between hospital and community care. The failure of communities to provide services and the scandal of homelessness is causing some social planners to rethink the issue. Under the doctrine of "least restrictive environment," established by a number of court cases, even the most severely disturbed can seldom be held in hospitals in most states unless they are a danger to themselves or others. Klein (1983), formerly with the Mental Health Law Project, a legal advocacy group with a strong commitment to keeping people out of hospitals, has now taken the position that the doctrine of least restrictive environment is fundamentally flawed. Treatment and liberty, he believes, cannot be treated as independent variables. Doing so places least restrictiveness as a higher value than safety and efficacy. Klein sees us now at a watershed on this issue, with the courts soon restoring commitment to a meaningful form of intervention aimed at treatment. There are, of course, strong countervailing forces against more extensive use of hospitals. Whether the ill person is spending long periods of time in the hospital or in the community affects the role that families play.

The question as to who is legally responsible for providing direct care is also a confusing issue. In the early days of deinstitutionalization, families assumed that care would be provided for by the state, as it once was when most patients were institutionalized. Klein (1983), however, says, "Regrettably, there is no legal right to services in our country. A legal right, as distinguished from a moral or ethical right, is one that is enforceable in court. There is no right to good housing. There is no right to adequate food. Indeed, despite many legal challenges in the later 1960's, it now appears generally accepted that there is no right to any largesse provided by the Constitution" (p. 108).

So who must take care of the mentally ill? At this time, no one is legally required to do so. In most states, relatives (other than spouses) are not being held legally responsible for the care of an adult relative. The presumption seems to be that as long as such adults are not involuntarily held, psychiatrically disabled persons are themselves responsible for their own care just as any other adult is in our society. But as we well know, many of these people cannot survive without support and supervision. Their survival depends on the ethical and moral, if not legal, commitment of others in society. Such moral commitment to the mentally ill has been limited, and unless families have come to the rescue, the disabled person has suffered.

Those who write about family intervention programs almost invariably lead off by quoting the figures of Minkoff (1978) or Goldman (1982), who report that approximately 65% of patients go home upon discharge from hospitals. More recently, Torrey and Wolfe (1986, p. iii) have provided the following information as to where our 2 million most seriously disturbed people live:

- 800,000 live with families.
- 200,000 live by themselves.
- 300,000 live in nursing homes.
- 300,000 live in foster homes, group homes, or other supervised settings.
- 200,000 are in hospitals.
- 26,000 are in jails.
- 150,000 live in public shelters and on the streets.

It is clear from these figures that families are responsible for a great deal of support and care, not for legal reasons, but because morally they feel they cannot choose to do otherwise. Many well meaning professionals use these figures to argue for more and better interventions with families. Such a direction might, then, make it a *fait accompli* that families be designated for that role. It is almost as though what is, is what ought to be. Some professionals, for example, Falloon et al. (1984), state or imply that families should be caregivers. Others, such as Torrey (1983) and Dincin (1975), feel that families should not do direct caregiving, for it is too stressful for both patient and family. But what do the families themselves think about this extended caregiving role?

The author circulated a brief questionnaire to attendees of the 1986 annual convention of the NAMI to ask two main questions: (1) What does the respondent believe would be the appropriate living arrangement for their relative? (2) If their relative had this appropriate living arrangement, what kind of help would the family need to cope with the stresses of mental illness on the family?

Of the 308 respondents to the questionnaire, nearly all were parents and over half were 60 years of age and over. Their mentally ill relative was most often male (78%) and 37% were living at home or under their family's supervision. With regard to the first question as to where families thought that their relative ought to live, the responses were as follows:

In the family home: 3%
In a minimally supervised community residence: 44%
In a highly supervised residence: 21%
Independently and/or minimally supervised by family: 32%
In a humane and supportive hospital or institution: 2%

In response to the second question as to what kinds of support and assistance families would need if their relative were in appropriate housing, respondents were allowed to check as many as applied. They responded as follows:

Respite services for the family: 18%
Twenty-four hour crisis availability: 49%
Advice and assistance from client's therapist: 64%
Short-term workshops, classes, and lectures: 43%
Intensive (1–2 years) training in management and problem-solving skills: 23%
Family therapy: 20%
No professional assistance to family would be needed: 25%

In conclusion, 95% of the respondents felt that their relative should be living in a community residence. Only a fifth of these families felt that their relative needed a highly supervised residence, with 76% favoring a minimally supervised or family-supervised residence. If these accommodations were available, families would still want considerable contact with the treating therapist and crisis availability. Short-term workshops and classes were significantly favored for families over more intensive and long-term kinds of treatment.

The belief that mentally ill adults should not be cared for in the family home was quite pronounced in the responses to the questionnaire. James Howe (1985), then president of the NAMI, argues that it is normal in our culture for adults to move out of the parental home to live among peers in the community, and that psychiatrically disabled people are more likely to persist in excessive dependent behaviors when they remain in childhood environments. At best, investment in training families is a short-lived solution, for parents of adult children are necessarily older, more prone to physical ailments, and destined to die before their disabled relative. Training families to be caregivers only delays the inevitable necessity of creating supportive residences in the community. These reasons and more probably explain family thinking about the inappropriateness of family care. Additional evidence of the NAMI groups' intentions is apparent in recent reports gathered from state and local affiliates, in which housing was by far the number one legislative goal.

Our best guess is that the amount of appropriate housing will increase at a modest rate over the next decade. It is unlikely that hospital stays will increase in length or number to any significant extent. We predict that many clients will be on waiting lists for a time, and families will provide direct care in the meantime. Families will want some help but their preferences will lie in short-term, educational approaches and in relying on the therapist treating their relative for ongoing advice and information. We know little about the intent and preferences of low-income families. This we need to know, for data seem to show that mental health professionals have been relatively unsuccessful in inferring what is needed and desired by families of the mentally ill (Hatfield, 1983; Holden & Lewine, 1982; McElroy, 1987).

Summary

In this chapter we have emphasized the necessity for mental health professionals to be alert to the current social and political factors that impinge on service delivery. While others might arrive at a somewhat different list, we identified five social factors that we felt had the most relevance to programs for families. Mainstream psychiatry now defines the mental illnesses as diseases or brain disorders that are unrelated to traditional mental health concerns. Hence, mental illness is becoming a field in its own right in which those who serve this population must be highly trained. As this new definition becomes fully understood, attitudes toward families will predictably change in a positive direction. While families are still major caregivers in most areas, family advocacy will likely result in a growth, though probably moderate, in available community housing. The shift will be slow enough that this generation of caregivers will still not see great relief. Thus, during this transitional period, many families will seek help and advice. Rather than special programs, or in addition to them, many families expect their relative's primary therapist to be an important source of information and advice. With a rapidly growing consumer movement, wise providers will enlist families in planning programs for families. Finally, it is necessary to consider how limited dollars can be most efficaciously used so that all those who desire help can get it. Fortunately, most families do not prefer the more costly and long-term kinds of assistance, but ideally such programs would be available for the minority who do want them.

CHAPTER 2

Mental Illness:
A Catastrophic Event

While stress is ubiquitous and a part of everyone's life, catastrophic levels of stress impact on people infrequently, and when they do, they do so powerfully and without warning. Mental illness is one of those catastrophic events that strikes infrequently, but when it does, it has devastating consequences for patients and families. Effective work with families requires that practitioners grasp the enormity of the stress placed on families and that they create models of help based on an empathic understanding of the family's dilemma.

While traditional theoretical models may have contributed to effective work with families in general, they contributed little to our understanding of how the family experiences mental illness. Neither psychoanalytic theory, various theories of communication deviance, family systems theory, nor expressed emotion theory have in any way led to better understanding of how families perceive and feel about mental illness. While each of these theories provided new ways of labeling and describing families, they did not enhance empathic understanding. Effective work with families depends upon full empathic understanding, and a new model is needed to lead us in that direction.

In an earlier work (Hatfield, 1987a), the author explored stress theory, and its broader context of coping and adaptation, to determine its usefulness as a theoretical framework for understanding the family response to mental illness. A review of relevant literature showed that this theory had excellent explanatory power for the effect of catastrophic events on people, and that it indeed served well to explain how families experience mental illness. The theory of coping and adaptation will guide the work in this volume, hence, with its basic concepts summarized briefly here. For those who wish to explore this framework more thoroughly, there is an abundant literature (e.g., see Coelho, Hamburg, & Adams, 1974; Figley & McCubbin, 1983; Hansell, 1976; Monat & Lazarus, 1977; Moos, 1976; Parad, 1965).

The theory of coping and adaptation starts with the assumption that all living systems strive to maintain themselves in their environment, to overcome obstacles, and to achieve autonomy and self-determination. The key concept "coping" is usually reserved for those efforts people must make to master conditions of threat, harm, or challenge when the usual strategies are insufficient. Therefore White's (1974) definition of coping suits our purposes well:

> It is clear that we tend to speak of coping when we have in mind a fairly drastic change or problem that defies familiar ways of behaving, requires the production of new behavior, and very likely gives rise to uncomfortable affects like anxiety, despair, guilt, shame or grief, the relief of which forms part of the needed adaptation. Coping refers to adaptation under relatively difficult circumstances. (pp. 48–49)

Families of the mentally ill face a drastic change in their lives, which requires significant changes in behavior and capacities for dealing with strong emotion. The bulk of this chapter will focus on the emotional trauma caused by mental illness and the chapter following it will describe the behavioral demands made upon the other family members.

A number of writers (Adler, 1982; Bruner & Connolly, 1974; Maluccio, 1981) use the term "competence" to describe the end goal of coping efforts. In this context, it involves selecting relevant information, having a planned course of action, and initiating a sequence of activities toward selected objectives. Success depends upon the ability to perform major social roles, maintain an adequate self-concept, manage strong affect, access available resources, manage developmental transitions, and maintain effective cognitive functioning (Adler, 1982). The relevance of these ideas to coping with mental illness will become apparent as we proceed.

The theory of coping and adaptation leads to different assumptions about family behavior and to different interpretations as to what is going on, in comparison to other family theories. While the emotional turmoil and confusion may be quite apparent in these families, older theorists assumed that these behaviors preceded the mental illness and caused it, thus leading to a diagnosis of family pathology. The literature on adaptation points out that people normally respond with strong affect and confusion when they encounter devastating events over which they have little control and little prior experience. Families see mental illness as a terrible family tragedy and believe their feelings of being overwhelmed by grief, anxiety, and remorse are quite appropriate to the trauma they are suffering. Through adaptation theory, professionals can come to understand families in a way that is empathic to them. Thus, the alienation of family from professional is less likely, and collaborative relationships are possible.

Newer developments in brain biology make it more possible to see mental illness as another chronic disabling physical illness that tends to stress relatives in a variety of ways. Coping and adaptation models serve well for understanding the dilemmas of families who face such severe and chronic diseases as cystic fibrosis, leukemia, muscular dystrophy, cerebral palsy, and Alzheimer's disease. It has never been assumed that family interaction patterns were a precursor to these disorders; rather we see these families as struggling to adapt to them. Likewise, as noted in Chapter 1, no individual or family style of behavior has been found to contribute to mental illness. Therefore, it is no longer possible to adhere to traditional family theories; moreover, it is incumbent upon us to develop conceptual models more appropriate to current thinking.

Regardless of whether the onset of mental illness is insidious or acute, the consequences for the family can border on disastrous. Sources of difficulty for the family are many and diverse, and they pervade nearly all aspects of existence, sometimes for a lifetime. Hoenig and Hamilton (1966) found it convenient to divide the burden of mental illness into two categories, which they called "subjective burden" and "objective burden." "Subjective burden" refers to the sense of anxiety, loss, grief, and pain caused by abnormal behavior in a member. Intrapsychic coping is required to come to terms with these painful feelings (Mechanic, 1974), which will be the focus of the rest of this chapter. "Objective burden" serves to describe the adverse effects on the household, such as heavy financial costs, negative effects on the health of others, and the disruption of lives. These problems require behavioral solutions that will be discussed in the next chapter.

The Onset of Mental Illness as a Crisis

The powerful emotional responses so apparent when mental illness strikes a member may be puzzling to some, or they may seem unnecessarily extreme to others. To those who have had mental illness in a close member, such strong feelings hold no surprises (Hatfield, 1978). The goal of this chapter is to analyze and explain family responses so that practitioners, too, can see these feelings as normal for a very abnormal situation.

The onset of mental illness invariably produces a state of crisis that in some ways is like any other severe crisis in life, and in other ways is quite unique in its consequences. A state of crisis occurs, Appley and Trumbull (1977) say, when a person meets a new, rapidly changing, difficult to comprehend chain of events for which the individual's usual range of experience does not prepare her or him. Note the following description of the onset of mental illness by Lefley (1987b), and the way it meets the definition of a crisis:

> Like the schizophrenic experience itself, the patient's decompensation generates in family members a fearful awareness of shifting ground and altered states of reality. The stricken person is no longer the same, and his unpredictable strangeness changes the world around him. In a psychotic state, he or she may be delusional, paranoid, aggressive, or manic. Displaced hostility or grandiosity may alternate with guilt for nameless crimes, profound depression, and suicide ideation. (p. 3)

Habitual problem-solving strategies are inadequate to these new realities, leaving the family anxious, bewildered, and overwhelmed.

Hirschowitz (1976), whose analysis adds to our understanding, prefers the term "transition states" to that of "crisis." "Transition" is marked by pattern disruption as the familiar reality gives way to a new kind of existence forced by some uncontrollable life event. So it is with families and mental illness when family members that were known and loved and for whom the future held great promise seem to have given way to different versions of themselves. The life that the family is accustomed to must give way to a style that can accommodate the inordinate demands of mental illness. Rapid adjustments must be made as each new development in the illness threatens the precarious stability that has been painfully achieved.

Psychological stress, Hirschowitz (1976) believes, is an expectable response to such demanding situations and should not be viewed as pathological. In catastrophic situations all aspects of existence are disrupted—psychological, physiological, and inter-personal. People are required to modify their identity, image, and roles, as well as face significant strangeness and the feeling of inescapability. Habitual patterns of response may become labored and difficult, and interactions with others may have an awkward quality with new role requirements only dimly perceived. Cognitive functioning may become paralyzed with a narrowing of perception and a tendency to look back with grief, anger, resentment, and guilt. Mental health professionals not fully aware of the nature of crisis reactions may easily assume family pathology, and, as in the past, assume that the family disorganization preceded and caused or precipitated the mental illness in a member.

Hansell (1976) rounds out our understanding of the crisis response through his concept of "being-in-distress." Some of the characteristics of "persons-in-distress" that are most apparent in families coping with mental illness are:

1. They show narrow, fixed spans of attention. There is a sense of urgency that "something must be done."
2. They report feeling alienated and alone. Their usual friends, family, and neighbors seem to have little importance for them.
3. There may be a profound sense of loss of identity.
4. There may be a drastically reduced capacity to make decisions.
5. They may perform their usual social roles in an unsatisfactory way.

Wrubel, Benner, and Lazarus (1981, pp. 80–84) have identified the characteristics of environments that place inordinate amounts of stress on people. Situational demands that tax adaptive capacity are:

1. *Uniqueness.* These are characteristics for which persons have had no previous experience to provide the necessary knowledge and skill, and for which the culture offers no patterns for response. For unpredictable events, no preparation is possible; people are caught off guard.

2. *Duration and frequency.* The length of time a demand is present influences the amount and degree of stress. Long durations of overload result in "burnout." "Frequency" refers to the repetition of discrete demands, each of which are time-limited but regularly repeated. The combination of long duration plus frequency of episode has particular potential for undermining people's coping resources. (It is not hard to see how mental illness, with

its long duration and cyclic exacerbations, plays such havoc on family life.) If duration seems indefinite and interminable, people often succumb to feelings of hopelessness.

3. *Pervasiveness.* When the situational demands permeate every corner of experience, one has the sense that every aspect of one's life is threatened or disturbed, and that there is no refuge.

4. *Ambiguity.* Some situations are highly explicit and structural. Their demands have great clarity; what is needed and expected is fairly obvious. It is much more difficult where there is confusion and ambiguity (as in mental illness)—ambiguity in terms of what is going on, what are appropriate role expectations, and what is the likely outcome.

Practitioners who work with families need to understand the state of crisis that almost invariably accompanies the onset of mental illness in a member. They need to be able to identify the behaviors that indicate families are suffering a severe reaction to an unacceptable reality. Shock, denial, helpless confusion, and escape are early responses to crises and are similar regardless of the source of the trauma. Beyond this, however, may be many and various emotional responses depending upon the interpretations of events by those who live with them. Mental illness has similarities with other tragedies in life, but there are also unique meanings because of the way mental illness presents itself.

The Meaning of Mental Illness to the Family

The clinical manifestations of the various mental illnesses are presented in great detail in the professional literature. The reality of mental illness for the research scientist or the college professor are the objective facts of these disorders—the nature of the brain's malfunctioning, the nature of the thinking disorders, the inappropriate moods, the incapacity for self-care or self-management of daily activities, the bizarre language, the tendencies to withdraw, and so forth. The objective reality of mental illness is certainly one of importance, but it is not the only one. There are other realities or ways of viewing mental illness for persons who suffer from mental disorders and still a different reality for those who care about the sufferer. Mental illness has many personal meanings for those it touches. The objective facts are given meaning by the personal interpretations assigned to them.

Theorists of coping and adaptation recognize the need to understand the interpretive function in crisis situations. Mechanic

(1974) believes that "students of coping and adaptation would do well to invest greater attention to the question of how men see their environment and their own potencies in meeting the challenges of the environment" (p. 37). In addition to objective reality, there is always a mediating, interpretative function going on. What is more, the interpretation is never static, but changes in quality and intensity as a function of new information and experiencing outcomes of previous responses (Appley & Trumbull, 1977). Lazarus (1977) sees the primary activity as that of appraisal. The individual makes judgments as to whether the effect of the event is likely to be harmful, beneficial, or irrelevant.

The concept of "threat" has been used to explain how people react to a potentially hazardous situation (Appley & Trumbull, 1977; Rapoport, 1965). The threat of harm produces negative affect, alterations in adaptive functioning, poor physiological states, and interpersonal conflicts. A threat to self-esteem or integrity will be met with anxiety; a threat to loss or deprivation will be met with depression (Rapoport, 1965). In addition, as Janis (1974) points out, the degree of threat depends on the amount of ego-involvement, the probability that the dangerous event will occur, the severity of loss if it does occur, and the probability of successful coping with whatever will happen.

We will examine the emotional impact of mental illness on the family in terms of the four major kinds of threat: (1) the threat of loss or deprivation; (2) the threat to self-esteem and self-worth; (3) the threat to security; and (4) the threat to integrity and hope. We will note that families suffer directly from these threats, but they suffer indirectly also through their empathic experience with their ill relatives' losses and threats to self-esteem and security.

The Threat of Loss and Deprivation

"Loss may be defined as a state of being deprived of or being without something one has had" (Peretz, 1970, p. 4). Losses may take many forms but the most profound is the loss of a significant or valued person. Peretz further points out that "the incapacitation of a valued person through acute or chronic illness may result in loss of some aspects of that person, such as a special quality or attribute which provides gratification" (p. 5).

Mentally ill people lose, temporarily or permanently, many of the personality characteristics that identify them. The change between the premorbid person and the personality affected by a serious brain disorder can be profound. It is as though one has lost a loved one through death, but mourning can never be complete since physically, at least, the person still lives. The cyclical nature of these disorders creates added difficulties: The family's hopes are raised as the patient improves, only to be dashed again as the illness resumes its course. Statements made by families illustrate the depth of grief: "I ache for her wasted life," wrote one sister. "Most of us feel our hearts have turned to stone. God only knows our anguish," said a father (Hatfield, 1978, p. 358).

Persistent sorrow is a frequent and overwhelming feeling. The potential of the individual will never be used. Broken dreams and shattered hopes for a loved family member must be given up, and there must be acceptance of the person as she or he is now. One close relative described her experience with the following words:

> It was really like a period of mourning, and I realized that it was. It was giving up the goals and the pictures of her as a normal adult functioning, working at a library, which had been her dream. I think that is what it was—giving up that picture of her as an adult. (Bernheim, Lewine, & Beale, 1982, p. 31)

Terkelsen (1987a) points out that unlike professionals, relatives have known an intact, whole person prior to the appearance of the illness. The parents of a strong, vibrant, young person will be especially agonized as the illness strips these talents away:

> It came as an utter and unbelievable surprise. We are all grieving for years now. We have watched a young life that was eager, healthy, attractive, with intelligence, humor and incisive sensitivity into human relationships, waste away, without any friends (when there were so many in the first twenty years), unable to stand any stress, being self-conscious and terrified, and almost never free from voices assailing him and sounds he cannot bear. (Terkelsen, 1987a, p. 137)

Especially painful, notes Lefley (1987a), are the ways in which mentally ill people distance themselves or shut off human contact. Although withdrawal may serve as a protective mechanism, families become exasperated when there is no response to a simple communication. They feel frustrated and rejected when they reach out and try to be supportive, only to find their overtures ignored or rebuffed. And they may find themselves feeling depleted as they continue to give so much and receive so little back. There is also the loss of the ill person's once important contribution to the life of the family, a gap in the family circle that is felt for a long time.

Many people who have mental disorders are painfully aware of the losses they have suffered because of mental illness. They know the poverty of their lives and the lost potential with which they must live. This is especially the case with those whose achievements and expectations were relatively high before the first illness episode. They grieve over these losses and their families empathically share their pain (Lefley, 1987a).

It is important that mental health professionals recognize the grieving reaction of families. The literature has been relatively silent about the grief and mourning of these families; therefore it is likely to be overlooked or misinterpreted as something else. Peretz (1970) describes in detail emotional reactions that may accompany loss: "The feelings and emotional states aroused by the loss of a loved one," he says, "include mental pain, yearning, anguish, sorrow, dejection, sadness, depression, fear, anxiety, nervousness, agitation, panic, anger, disbelief, denial, shock, numbness, relief, emptiness, and lack of feeling" (p. 13). The individual may have feelings of resentment and anger toward the loved one, but may have trouble accepting these feelings and as a consequence experience guilt and shame. The person may dwell upon the past and recall how good things once were, or she or he may recall presumed omissions or failures.

Intense grief reactions may include the following symptoms: tightness in the throat, shortness of breath, sighing, loss of appetite, and loss of sleep. They may also include manifest subjective distress, depression, uncontrolled crying, and debilitating anxiety, and there may be a sense of helplessness, hopelessness, and despair (Bugen, 1980). Predicting the length of a grief reaction is difficult, but from the work of Wikler, Wasow, and Hatfield (1981) on mental retardation, it appears that a less intense but persistent chronic sorrow normally will last indefinitely.

Belief about the preventability or unpreventability of a death also influences the intensity and duration of a grief reaction. Preventability means that there were factors contributing to the death that could have been controlled, or that the survivors themselves contributed to the death either directly or indirectly. Unpreventability refers to the belief that nothing could be done (Bugen, 1980). The parallel with the preventability or unpreventability of mental illness is obvious. To the extent that families believe that mental illness is a brain disease not presently understood or preventable, grief is lessened. To the extent that mental illness is thought to be on a continuum with lesser adjustment problems, families feel guilty for not recognizing early symptoms and aborting a full-blown disorder.

We have culturally provided customs and rituals for easing the pain of those who have lost someone through death, whereas little cultural support is provided to ease the pain of those who have lost someone through mental illness. Finding ways to help families through their intense bereavement process is a challenge to mental health professionals.

The Threat to Self-Esteem and Self-Worth

In working with people facing severe adaptational challenges, self-esteem must be maintained at all cost, and, whenever possible, must be enhanced. There must be left intact a sense of competence and an inner assurance that one can do things necessary for a satisfactory life. Loss of a satisfactory self-image leads to anxiety, shame, and guilt (White, 1974).

Goldschmidt (1974) argues that it is human nature to be concerned with maintenance of self-esteem and a positive self-image, and that human beings are probably preprogrammed toward self-interested, status-oriented behavior that has survival value for them. One gets self-esteem from culturally valued successes in life and positive recognition from others. For instance, in this country people expect to get considerable ego-gratification from raising their children to become successful adults. The sacrifices that parents make over a long period of child rearing ordinarily have their rewards by having upstanding, competent adult children to point to with pride. What happens, then, to the self-image of parents whose children have severe mental illnesses and who may never fulfill the role of the "successful parent"?

EMBARRASSMENT AND SHAME

The very symptoms by which people are diagnosed as having a mental illness are sources of shame to many parents. In acute stages, mentally ill people may appear bizarre to those around them. They may verbalize strange delusions of thought insertion or thought control; they may act on grandiose schemes or propound great religious ideation; they may say they hear things not heard by others; they may show poor judgment and dress in attention getting clothing and neglect personal hygiene, and so forth. In other words, they "act as though something is wrong with them"; they act "crazy," and families invariably react with shame.

The social skills of mentally ill persons may be lacking and their attempts at social contact clumsy. Families may dread having visitors at home and feel conflicted about taking the impaired person to a restaurant or theater. Lefley (1987a) illustrated this problem with the following vignette:

> A 17-year-old schizophrenic young man makes clumsy sexual advances to the girlfriends of his 12-year-old sister. The friends are afraid to come to her house and the child is agonized with embarrassment, and in danger of losing her peer group. The parents do not know how to treat the situation or how to instruct the young girl on what she should say to her friends. (p. 115)

Another mother related her profound embarrassment as she told the following story to the author:

> A young couple from Germany, former friends of the family, dropped in unannounced for a short visit. The visitors were unaware that some profound changes had occurred in that family in the past 3 years. They were soon to know. The 21-year-old son and his girlfriend, both in acute stages of schizophrenia, swept in. Both were wearing highly outlandish costumes with strange layers of clothing and color clash. The girlfriend had thick layers of makeup, a very short skirt, and huge combs in her long hair. The mother caught her breath and introduced them to the guests. The son bowed low over the female visitor's hand, kissed it, and murmured "Enchanté. Enchanté." The son and girlfriend soon left, the mother could find no words to explain the situation, and the visitors departed with puzzled expressions on their faces. (E. Peterson, personal communication, November 10, 1985)

How do families maintain their sense of self-worth in the face of such bizarre events, and what can helping professionals realistically offer by way of constructive help to families in handling such circumstances?

Furthermore, as Lefley (1987a) states so well, "One of the most devastating sequelae of mental illness is the reaction to one's own deviance. Many can sometimes see their own 'craziness' through others' eyes" (p. 111). In addition, Lefley believes that the dysfunctional mentally ill are acutely aware of their lack of skills, impaired productivity, and poor future potential. Thus, families not only suffer directly because of their relative's strange behaviors; they also suffer empathically because of their relative's shame and embarrassment.

To maintain or regain a sense of self-esteem depends upon actual success in coping with the problems presented. The management of a household in which a member is floridly psychotic presents a challenge with which few can cope at first. As families so often say, "Nothing seems to work." What parents learned in raising their other children just does not seem to apply in this situation. There is considerable floundering, grasping for new answers, and failure after failure before some sense of direction develops. "He never learns," said one mother. "He makes the same mistakes over and over again" (Hatfield, 1978, p. 359).

The support of others—lay and professional—is needed to help the mentally ill acquire the information and develop the skills for successful mastery. Sharing experiences can lessen the sense of burden and provide role models of others who have surmounted similar turmoil. Personal worth can be reinforced by the care and concern exhibited by professionals or by the natural network of friends and relatives. "No adaptive strategy that is careless of self-esteem is likely to be any good," advises White (1976, p. 31), and Hansell (1976) notes that "Self-esteem breathes oxygen into the painful unchartered journey of meeting an adaptational change" (p. 42).

As our concept of support and education develops in this book, we will demonstrate that professionals can play an important role in reaffirming the sense of self-worth in family members who have lost it through the exigencies of mental illness. The theories we hold, the language we use, and our attitudes and needs make an important difference.

GUILT AND BLAME

Mental illnesses are the only disorders that have culturally transmitted hypotheses of family pathogeneses—as etiological agents or as precipitants (Lefley, 1987b). Although blaming families as causal agents in their relative's illness is now considered rather archaic, considering them as precipitants of relapse has gained in credibility. Those involved in expressed emotion theory or related concepts have not explained how they can prevent families and patients from avoiding a sense of failure when there is relapse.

Recently families seem to have shed some of their guilt that they cause mental illness. This Lefley (1987b) sees as "a salutary advance perhaps due to the maturation of the field and to the development of the family movement" (p. 7). Nevertheless, Lefley still sees families suffering from a considerable amount of self-blame: They feel culpability for behaviors that may have in some ways triggered decompensation if not the disorder itself; they feel guilty about hostile feelings toward the patient even though they may be legitimate responses to provocative or intolerable behavior; they may feel guilty about leaving a loved one in unpleasant and sometimes hated surroundings when the family itself has a pleasant home; and they may feel guilty when they make more self-protective life decisions for themselves.

Because all child rearing is accompanied by mistakes of lesser or greater intensity, families of the mentally ill may hark back to things that have happened—short tempers, physical punishment, harsh words, and so forth. They may suffer remorse over divorce in the family or the death of an important member. Families in this country grow up with a sense of omnipotence, of being able to control fate and guarantee the future of their children. This idea is constantly supported by the textbooks with which professionals are trained, by messages conveyed by practitioners to families, and by the popular culture, which has fed on this tenet.

Guilt leads to depression and robs people of self-confidence and self-worth. It paralyzes them in their efforts to cope, leading to cycles of unsuccessful coping and more guilt. Guilty people, note Bernheim and colleagues, are more likely to martyr themselves needlessly, to make endless self-sacrifices that in turn make the patient feel guilty and burdened with a debt of gratitude to his family. Guilt makes it difficult to set limits and to determine a helpful level of involvement with the patient (Bernheim & Lehman, 1985; Bernheim et al., 1982).

STIGMA

One of the earliest studies of the consequences of mental illness to the family, that of Clausen and Yarrow (1955), reported that the dynamics of social and psychological situations of these families and their mechanisms of adjustment in many ways paralleled those of minority groups. Feelings were characterized by a sense of underprivilege and marginality, and they displayed hypersensitivity to the facts of mental illness and had a strong need to conceal it.

"Stigma [is] an ugly word and an ugly reality for many patients and their families," states Flynn (1987). "The stigma of mental illness is often as painful and disabling as the symptoms of major psychiatric disorders" (p. 53). Stigma is a mark of disgrace for those whom society brands as deviant. For the patient it means a constant series of rejections and exclusions. Families take on stigma as a shared burden with their relatives. They think carefully about whom to tell about the disorder, and, at times spend much energy contriving to conceal it.

Rabkin (1984) has reviewed the research on public attitudes toward mental illness. She reports that openly expressed negative attitudes toward the mentally ill have declined over time. It is no longer socially acceptable to exclude those who are labeled mentally ill. However, people are still apprehensive about their unpredictable behavior and possible dangerousness. In general, the label of mental illness continues to have negative connotations, although Rabkin believes that the negative attitudes are more toward the deviant behavior than the illness itself. However, deviant behavior does characterize much mental illness for much of the time; thus, mental illness is still a closet disease for many patients and their families. Given families' perception of mental illness as stigmatizing, we must help them find constructive ways to deal with it.

The Threat to Security

To feel secure in their environment, people must see themselves as physically safe, able to predict events, and able to exert some control over them. They react to insecurity with anxiety and tension. Families of the mentally ill report that they suffer high and persistent levels of anxiety (Hatfield, 1983). Anxiety, say Bernheim and Lehman (1985), may be a consuming, ever-present sensation. Families may wake up in the morning with apprehension for what the day may bring, or even dread what they may need to face. Johnson (1984) simply says, "Life with schizophrenia is life at the raw edges of existence" (p. 47).

DANGEROUSNESS

There are constant fears that the mentally ill person may hurt himself or others. Suicide threats or attempts leave families on edge. Typically reflecting poor impulse control, people with mental illnesses may direct hostility toward family members because of jealousy, hypersensitivity to criticism, or perceived obstruction of desires (Lefley, 1987a). Carelessness with cigarettes, unwillingness to seek medical or dental care, susceptibility to attack by others in the street all add to the families' burden of anxiety.

Some mentally ill people wander or find themselves homeless on the streets. To have one's vulnerable relative in the hostile climate of an urban street is the culmination of a family's worst fears. By virtue of their imagination and stories in the local press, families envision unremitting cold, hunger, filth, fatigue, and loneliness. It is sheer agony to think about what may happen to her or him. The following is the account of one such distraught mother:

> Mrs. A has not seen her son, John, for six months and wonders if he is alive or dead. John split from the hospital he was in, and no one has heard from him since. The last time Mrs. A. caught sight of him was when she was on her way to work downtown and noticed a person who resembled John out of the corner of her eye. She stopped the car and shouted, "John it's me . . . Mom." John looked up, called her a "God-damned bitch" and bolted into the alley. She said he looked like a beggar, unclean and ragged.
>
> Mrs. A. still searches for John. Sometimes from her car window she sees someone about the right build and she calls, "John, is that you?" It never is. She makes the rounds of the medical examiner's offices in Baltimore, and she checks out accident or homicide victims who have ended up at the morgue. One might be John. If she hears about unclaimed bodies of young men who have washed up on the beach, she checks that out too. She has not found him. She said, "I don't know if it would be easier to know that he was dead or not. At least it would be over, and I wouldn't be watching for him." (Hatfield, Farrell, & Starr, 1984, p. 283)

Not only are families fearful for their relatives, they are also sometimes afraid of them. The frequency with which mentally ill people assault their own families has not been widely studied, hence, the importance of a recent study by Swan and Lavitt (1986) of 1156 members of the National Alliance for the Mentally Ill (NAMI) in which the family's experience with patient violence was assessed. Over one-third of the families reported that their ill relative was assaultive and destructive in the home either sometimes or frequently. In addition, it is quite probable that many families, although never assaulted, live in fear of their relative, and thus guard their behavior and create such protective measures as locks on doors and hiding of sharp instruments.

It is also possible that some family members are highly anxious about their own possible loss of control. Mentally ill people can be so manipulative, hostile, argumentative, and provocative that even the most controlled persons may feel that they could strike out in fear or anger.

UNPREDICTABILITY

Schizophrenia and mood disorders are highly unpredictable disorders. Exacerbations tend to be cyclical, but their exact pattern may never become apparent. This means that families cannot plan for the next episode and find themselves jolted into action at the most inconvenient times. Families soon learn to stay on guard, to live in apprehension that the shoe will soon drop again. There is no escape from being constantly on the alert. There is no knowing how the next episode will present itself, what strange dilemmas will occur, or what capacities families must find in themselves to survive the next round of events. At best, it may take years before the patient's episodes show some predictability and families build up a repertoire of coping responses that are serviceable to them.

The future course of a mental illness is unpredictable. Will the person improve or get worse? When will be the next relapse? Will the family be able to manage it successfully? In addition, siblings and children of mentally ill persons fear for their futures and the possibilities of genetic transmission to themselves or their offspring.

Parents of mentally ill people assume that they will predecease their relative, a thought that is almost too painful to contemplate for some. Who will care for their disabled family members when they die? Will they be in the streets? Maltreated? Lonely? Or will the system respond and see that the ill are cared for?

Mental illness is a costly disease. Good insurance coverage is not available. Dwindling financial resources is a constant worry. It is difficult to balance the needs of all family members and even more difficult to plan for future eventualities—retirement, illness, and death.

LACK OF POWER

Families often feel that they carry a great deal of responsibility but have little power to influence things. The rights of adult patients to make their own decisions about treatment, hospitalization, and money leaves families in a terrible quandary when bad decisions are made. Patients may make these decisions, but they often cannot or do not take responsibility for them. Thus, the family feels it has no choice but to do so.

Families sometimes do not understand mental illness and its treatments and become, therefore, victims of exploitive practices of some professionals. Families are pressured into placing the patient in treatment programs that the family feels are ill-advised. Coercive measures are used to persuade families that the patient will not get well if a certain treatment is not undertaken (Johnson, 1987). "Family members have discovered that the urgency of these treatments ceases," Johnson notes, "when the families' economic resources are exhausted" (p. 74).

When zealous practitioners become especially eager that the patient do better or avoid relapse, the situation is ripe for scapegoating. Since outcomes for mentally ill people are tenuous at best, professionals may find themselves frustrated at their lack of success and begin blaming families for "overprotecting" or "sabotaging" the plan. Professionals may ignore the fact that it is the patient, her- or himself, who retains most of the control over the situation.

The Threat to Integrity and Optimism

The onset of mental illness in a loved one with its shattered hopes and dreams may bring with it a crisis of confidence in the world, a loss of faith in the universe, and the painful reality of human fragility and vulnerability. Stearns (1984), in a small book entitled *Living Through Personal Crises*, shares much wisdom about loss and how people respond. In his opinion, people may feel angry about the unfairness of life and may feel angry at the person who is lost for being the cause of their pain. They may feel angry at those who do not understand their pain and who seem so safe, secure, and distant from it all. They may feel angry at the universe, or at God, for letting this terrible tragedy happen. Their long held religious beliefs may be put to a test.

It is difficult to release our unrealistic expectations about what life ought to be, such as that it should be more fair and that there should be less suffering. "Life is what it is," Stearns tells us. "We are all vulnerable and needful people. In human life fairness has nothing to do with illness, death, divorce, accidents, shattered dreams and a host of other losses. The world cannot be what we want it to be" (p. 178).

People do recover from their losses and go on with life. "Our losses change us and change the course of our lives. It is not that one can never again be happy following an experience of loss. The reality is simply that one can never again be the same" (Stearns, 1984, p. 26). People find strengths inside themselves previously unknown to them. They lose their sense of innocence and omnipotence and are more aware of life as it is.

Through time people cease asking why this happened to them, knowing, finally, that life can be that way. It is then possible to face the questions of what to do about it. Lefley (1987c) sums up what that might mean:

> Coming to terms involves acceptance of the illness without loss of hope; laying to rest vestigial questions of cause and agency, and the accompanying fantasies of changed life events; learning to control one's own reactions to aversive behavior, including the option to move away from it; resolving obligations to the patient, to other family members, and particularly oneself. To attain this level of strength takes knowledge and learning of new adaptive strategies. (p. 16)

Given our lengthy description of the painful dilemmas that families must face and Lefley's (1987c) long list of adaptive changes that families must make, the remarkable thing is that most families do come to terms with mental illness and develop the competence to deal with the problems presented. For many, however, it takes a very long time. We believe that this tortuous path to acceptance can be less painful and possibly shortened for families if they have the support of professionals as well as relatives and friends. To this end we have tried to raise the level of awareness of professional helpers in this chapter. Later, we will discuss the concept of support and how it might best be provided to families of the mentally ill.

Summary

We have shown that the onset of mental illness in a relative rivals most other human catastrophes in terms of its consequences for the rest of the family. For those seeking a conceptual framework for a better understanding of the dilemma of the family in these circumstances, we recommend the theory of coping and adaptation, which emphasizes that the responses of families are understood as their best attempts to adapt to a painful new reality. The onset of mental illness represents a crisis to the family, and as the shock and dismay subside, families must deal with a great array of painful emotions. It may take a long time until some degree of acceptance can be achieved. Crucial to this process is the quality of support these families receive.

CHAPTER 3

Meeting Environmental Challenges

The process of adapting to a severe mental illness in a relative not only requires coming to terms with painful emotional experiences, it also involves rapid adjustments to complex and poorly understood patient behaviors. As Kanter (1985) clearly demonstrated in his recent work, there are no easy answers. It may require months and even years before the family has a handle on the problems of their troubled relative. Progress depends upon the severity of behavioral manifestations of the illness, the energies and capabilities of the family, and the kinds of support it receives. The concomitants of mental illness constantly call upon the family to do something—to make decisions, solve problems, and take action. Yet little of the ordinary experiences of living in a family prepare its members for the unusual behaviors presented by mental illness.

For purposes of discussion, we first note problems presented in meeting the needs of patients as they attempt to live with their impairments, then we identify problems that families face as they try to maintain a stable environment for the rest of the family. Finally, we discuss competence and self-efficacy as the end goals of the adaptive process for patient and family.

Meeting the Needs of All Family Members

Helping Patients

The onset of mental illness has a painful and disorganizing effect on patients as they try to make sense out of their environment and struggle to adjust to a world that now seems very strange to them.

Close relatives observe the painful dilemma endured and search for ways to respond to these seemingly intractable problems.

DIFFICULTY IN SELF-REGULATION

Excesses in smoking, eating, and sleeping are common complaints of families, who are baffled by their relatives' failure to exercise control over these functions and worry about consequences to health. Some patients may shower and change clothes only under duress; others may tie up the bathroom by insisting on several showers a day. Attitudes toward possessions may take excessive directions: They may spend money immediately and frivolously or refuse to part with a penny; they may hoard everything they find or carelessly lose or destroy whatever they have; they may be adamant about what is appropriate to wear or be totally indifferent to their appearance. These excesses are difficult for others to live with, and they seriously interfere with a person's adjustment to life. Families may search endlessly for responses that would reduce their persistence.

CONFLICT BETWEEN DEPENDENCE AND INDEPENDENCE

Families are frequently concerned about the amount of protection and support to provide in the face of their ill relatives' seeming ambivalence about being dependent on others. Families observe their relatives showing little initiative in solving their own problems, turning to their families with postures of helplessness, and seeming not to learn from experience. Yet when their families do attempt to regulate or advise them, they may be enraged and accuse them of controlling them or running their lives. Lefley (1987a) aptly describes this dilemma: "Anger directed at the mother reflects the conflict of one who wants to move away from the life buoy, but is afraid of drowning. Yet if the parent removes the buoy, the child may indeed drown or else flounder so miserably that his progress is significantly impeded" (p. 120).

Professionals often accuse families, especially parents, of overprotecting their relatives or having a pathological need to keep them dependent. Professionals who have not had day-to-day experiences with these ambivalent patient behaviors may fail to appreciate how difficult it is to titrate the appropriate amount of protection and support and yet allow for enough risk taking to permit growth. Families feel the need to prevent their relatives from doing things ruinous to their future or that will involve their families in expensive and time-consuming rescue operations. It is a difficult tightrope to walk.

PERSISTENT AVOIDANCE OF THREATENING SITUATIONS

People with mental illnesses spend much time and effort avoiding ordinary life situations because they find them threatening. Rather than reaching out, confronting new situations, and learning to cope with new realities, they use all their energies to find ways to avoid them. As one mother stated, "He [the patient] seems to have given up on life—he just wants to eat and sleep" (Hatfield, 1978, p. 356). Some of these people are exquisitely sensitive to threats to their self-esteem. They anticipate failure and fear rejection. Their anxieties run high, sometimes to panic proportions, and they are unable to devise strategies for anxiety management. Constant fear and anxiety breed fatigue, with resignation, despair, and avoidance the results. Unfortunately, avoidance keeps patients from moving forward and developing potentially rewarding experiences. Their families may grieve over this waste of life, but find it difficult to know when to nudge, nag, or pressure.

SOCIAL ISOLATION

Families worry about the lonely state of their relatives, often pointing out that they do not have a single friend. Sometimes they blame the stigma of mental illness and other people's indifference, but they often sadly note that their relative is not very rewarding to be around. The person may contribute little to the conversation, have difficulty concentrating on what is being said, fail to reciprocate favors and gifts, and otherwise act in inappropriate or even bizarre ways. Families are baffled when faced with decisions as to how they might play a role in strengthening their ill relative's social life.

SELF-DESTRUCTIVE BEHAVIORS

Not only do many mentally ill people risk self-destruction through severe eating problems, smoking, carelessness with fire, and failure to treat injuries and illnesses; they are also susceptible to drug and alcohol abuse, and a significant percentage are actively suicidal. Some families endure long periods constantly on guard, fearful that the next tragic event in the family might be severe injury or death.

Families have the burden of sorting out what they can do and what they cannot do to improve the lot of their ill relative. Furthermore, they must define how much they will give of themselves, what behaviors they will tolerate, and how much time and energy they will invest. While families can learn techniques that will be helpful to their relatives, Lefley (1987a) cautions against unrealistic expectations of them. She says:

> Familial coping with mental illness requires a shedding of rescue fantasies that in a great part have been nurtured by professionals. It is grandiose for families to believe that they have caused or can cure a phenomenon as awesome as mental illness. They can only try to modify their behavior to make life more comfortable for themselves and their mentally ill relatives. (p. 121)

Balancing the Needs of All Members

In spite of the tragedy of mental illness for those who are its victims, life must go on. Families find themselves needing to reconstruct life so that, not only are they accommodating the patient's special needs, but there is normality and growth for other family members. That this becomes a challenge of inordinate proportions will become clear as we describe some of the intrusive behaviors exhibited by highly disturbed individuals.

EXPLOITIVE AND PROVOCATIVE BEHAVIOR

For reasons not easily explained, once well-behaved individuals can be indescribably difficult to live with after the onset of mental illness. Possibly in an effort to achieve some kind of control over their confused and unfulfilling lives, these people can become highly exploitative and demanding of their families. Unproductive arguments may abound. Family tensions may rise. Some patients are acutely aware of their parents' areas of vulnerability and they use that knowledge to break down parental resistance and get their demands met. To be falsely accused of being tightfisted, uncaring, insensitive, or selfish may well succeed in getting well-meaning parents to capitulate to the unreasonable demands of their manipulative relative. Concomitantly, families may feel helpless and angry at the power their disturbed relative has over others. Disturbed persons, Kanter (1985) observes, have an amazing capacity to control their environments.

HOSTILE AND ABUSIVE BEHAVIOR

Families live in a continual state of anxiety wondering when the next outbreak of anger will occur. When families attempt to set limits to negative behaviors, patients often angrily cite their civil rights and accuse their families of totalitarian tactics. Families end up feeling tyrannized (Kanter, 1985), with some living in fear that the disturbed person may lose control and assault someone. These families approach issues gingerly and, when in doubt, may placate rather than risk a confrontation. They feel helpless and resentful, a victim of their relative's illness.

Families are surely confused as to whether these threatening behaviors are mad (i.e., sick), or bad. To what extent are these behaviors due to uncontrollable impulses and to what extent does the individual know what she or he is doing? There are no definitive answers as to where the line of accountability for actions can be drawn. Nevertheless, we believe that most mentally ill people have it within their power to modify their actions and develop behaviors conducive to living with others. Families can learn to enforce basic limits so that their safety, privacy, and comfort are maintained.

INVASION OF PRIVACY

Some family members find that the greatest difficulty is in not having any privacy. Whether they are on the telephone, taking a shower, or having a quiet conversation with another, they are in constant jeopardy of being interrupted. Some patients have little ability to delay gratification and go to any lengths to get their needs met. Patients living elsewhere feel they should be able to call home or drop in whenever it suits them. They do not easily put themselves in other people's shoes and, therefore, do not understand how annoying these interruptions can be.

USE OF POOR JUDGMENT

Difficulty in making reasoned decisions and judgments is certainly a part of these illnesses, with considerable consequences for others. Waste of money and other resources, breakage of furniture and equipment, sexual entanglements, and legal difficulties plague most families with disturbed relatives. The right of mentally ill people to make their own decisions is well protected in our society. Unfortunately, these people are not always able or willing to take responsibility for these decisions, and the consequences of them weigh heavily on others, most often their families.

We have identified just some of the wide array of difficulties that may be presented by mental illness. Even a brief experience with a family will reveal an enormous list of behavioral problems that may need to be faced on a day-by-day basis. However, families do learn to manage. Through a long, dynamic, evolving, unending process, they become increasingly competent with the problems presented. It is useful to understand this drive to competence, which seems to be inherent in people so that assistance and support to families can be most effective.

The Drive to Competence

Adaptation theory maintains the optimistic view that all people have the potential for growth and an innate propensity for environmental competence and mastery. Families of the mentally ill strive for competence in the face of overwhelming environmental demands. "The competent individual," we are informed by Ford (1985, p. 5), "is one who has successfully adapted to a given set of personal and contextual goals, demands, and opportunities." To reach an adequate level of competence depends upon the development of problem-solving skills and the ability to take effective and timely action. An abundance of knowledge and information is needed, satisfactory internal conditions must be maintained, and a sense of self-efficacy or empowerment must be pervasive. Adaptive mechanisms and coping strategies are creations that families themselves make, but professionals can help by providing information, helping to develop problem-solving skills, and giving support. How to provide such help is discussed in later chapters.

Reintegration of the Family Unit

Much of the literature on coping with a handicapped family member has focused on strategies that individual members have used. In this section, we will focus on the family as a unit and the adjustments required over time in altering family member roles, adjusting operations within the household, altering social activity and leisure time, and finding new ways to meet the diverse needs of all family members. Families face difficult moral and ethical decisions as they try to reach a delicate balance between the imperatives of their ill members' treatment and the needs of other children in the family, elderly parents, and the like.

How well the family copes as a unit depends in part on the range of life stressors that come its way in addition to the catastrophic stresses of mental illness. Selye (1956) and Holmes and Rahe (1967) have demonstrated that an array of human events ranging from the death of a spouse, loss of a job, arrival of a new baby, move to a new residence, and so forth, all add up to a sum total of stress that can result in severe psychosomatic distress and illness. Families of the mentally ill are, of course, just as vulnerable to these stresses as other families, and these stressors are added to the overwhelming stress of mental illness. There has been little research interest in understanding the physical and mental price families of the mentally ill must pay. Common sense suggests that it must be severe and that many families are at risk. This knowledge must be foremost as we consider the kinds of help to offer.

There is no single best way for families to reorganize and adapt to meet the demands of mental illness. Professionals who come to this work with rigid concepts of how all families must function may do more harm than good. What Kazak and Marvin (1984) say about functioning in families of handicapped children in general is instructive to those who work with the mentally ill. "Successful, adaptive functioning in families with handicapped children has not received sufficient attention. In their well-intentioned efforts to document areas of difficulty in families with handicapped children, researchers have sometimes neglected to describe ways in which differences may indicate successful family functioning within a *different but not deviant family structure*" (pp. 67–68, italics added). The implications for professionals are considerable, a point that will be made repeatedly throughout this book. Many of the family interventions of the past have been narrowly conceived, oblivious to the wide range of cultural differences in this country, and laden with personal values as to how all "normal" families should behave. It is in the hope of broadening perspectives that we introduce the topics of the role adjustment required to accommodate an ill member, the importance of the developmental stage of the family unit and its members, and the importance of culture.

Family Member Roles

We begin with the premise of Hill (1986) that "since the family is an interdependent system, change in the role content of one specific position brings changes in other roles" (p. 20). When a person becomes mentally ill, then, there is inevitably a shift in roles due to the loss of role function of the mentally ill person. How that shift is made depends on the role formerly played: wife–mother, husband–father, adult–child, or child of a mentally ill parent. In addition to the loss of role function, there is a drain in energy required for the caretaking. Well members of the family have normal needs for nurturance, stimulation, or supervision. They may feel neglected and become resentful of the disturbed member. Hence, considerable family reorganization is required if all needs are to be met.

The style that the new organization takes will vary considerably from family to family. There is no ideal pattern to recommend to all. What is important is that there is a fair and equitable division of tasks and a fair allocation of resources within the family unit, that members contribute according to their level of competence, and that the emerging needs of each are met. This is no small task and can only be approximated when the impairments of the ill person are severe.

Reorganization may also require a redefinition of relationships with those outside of the household. Families often find that they have to adapt to the time and energies they have left and limit their social contacts. They may need more from their social networks than they can contribute, and they may find that they no longer have much by way of common interests and activities that they can share. Sometimes extended families can be counted on since they may demand less by way of reciprocity. Some social isolation may be a necessary accommodation. Not understanding the family dilemma, professionals have interpreted social isolation as evidence of family pathology and as a precursor to mental illness rather than an adaptation to it.

The Family Life Cycle

When a mental illness occurs in a family, it occurs at a definite stage in the family's life cycle. The reaction of the family may be quite different if a parent becomes impaired in the early years of launching a family, during the period of adolescent children, or in later years. At each stage of the life cycle there are challenges as well as potentials for gratification. In addition to meeting these normal challenges, families who have an impaired member must create their own adaptation to life given what mental illness has dealt them.

The occurrence of mental illness in a parent seriously complicates the rearing of children and the marital relationship. The remaining parent must bear the total burden of child care, home-making, and bringing in money. The couple may be continually on the brink of separation or may divorce as a solution. The usual upset of adolescence may become more stressful as these children are torn between premature separation or spending their youth with heavy responsibilities. As they grow older they may feel guilty about leaving home and establishing an independent life.

If the onset of mental illness is in young adulthood, then we are talking about families in late middle age. This is the period when children typically leave home and the couple begins rediscovering each other. The presence of a disabled member may result in the loss of intimacy, sexual life, and shared activities. The couple's social life may be so restricted that they lose relationships with other less encumbered friends. Parents may find themselves caught with responsibilities to elderly parents as well as to the mentally ill offspring. It is not unusual for a parent—usually the mother—to be anxiously dividing her time between a dying mother in Florida and a decompensating son or daughter at home in Pennsylvania.

Parents may have difficulty defining and perhaps justifying the dependent role of the impaired offspring. They are under pressure to find ways for this person to have a role in the family, and to avoid despair and hopelessness as siblings go forward to graduation, marriage, and achievement. In addition, they are under pressure to help them adjust as siblings redefine their relationship to the disabled person, as they establish careers and make homes of their own.

In the final stages of life—retirement and old age—taking responsibility for a mentally ill person predictably becomes much more difficult. With the dearth of community resources, many of the psychiatrically disabled have become the responsibility of aging parents. The developmental specialists say that the primary task of old age is to review and accept the events of one's life history and to find meaning in it all. This presents a unique challenge to parents of mentally ill offspring whose deepest hopes have been so seriously aborted. Another task of this period is to come to terms with death, but these parents have an additional burden—what will happen to their relative when they are gone. In their worst imaginings, she or he will be lonely, destitute, and uncared for.

Although the elderly vary considerably in their rate of decline, some loss of strength and stamina is inevitable as is the possibility of a chronic illness or disability. The heart handles stress less well and takes longer to return to normal. The circulatory system becomes less efficient as artery walls thicken and the lungs have less efficiency. Senses are usually less acute, reaction time slower, and sleep less restorative. The body and mind pressure the older person to slow down (Newman & Newman, 1975; Schell & Hall, 1979). Hence, as Schell and Hall (1979) note, the older person is at special risk in the face of stress:

> Older people are particularly affected by the close relationship between stress and disease. . . . Because major life stresses and changes tend to pile up in later adult years, it is more likely that the older individual's abilities to handle change may be tested beyond his limits and that a serious and even terminal illness may result. (p. 466)

During any stage of the family cycle, a single-parent household is at a disadvantage. Hanson and Sporakowski (1986) found that the rate is much higher among blacks than whites. Single-parent households are usually headed by women who are disadvantaged economically, as well as with regard to education and mobility. The single parent has many more roles to play with attendant physical and emotional stress. Having a disabled person as a member of the household, then, can lead to burnout for the one who shoulders the responsibility alone.

Cultural Differences

This is a country of vast cultural differences, but we know very little about the effect of mental illness on culturally different families. The lack of research in this area puts the provider at a great disadvantage. In order to provide culturally relevant help, we need to be open to many patterns of response to mental illness in a member. There is no ideal that applies to all. Important to understand are the ways that various members of the family relate to each other—husband to wife, parents to children—and what their expected roles and obligations are to each other. In the wider kinship arena, there are in-law and intergenerational relationships and expectations that are important to know. Also important to know is the role of religion, the predominant value systems, the degree of geographic mobility, and attitudes toward work and achievement. All of these affect the meaning of mental illness for the family and the ways in which the family will organize around it.

We may have much to learn from nonindustrialized countries, for there is some evidence that mental illnesses run a less severe course in some of them. They may be less achievement-oriented than Western cultures, and thus provide a more benign climate for the adjustment of a psychiatrically disabled member. More meaningful, but less stressful work, may be available in villages and on small farms. In countries like China, Nigeria, and the Philippines, society is less likely to blame the family or patient. Families are usually seen as a supportive asset to the mentally ill, and may in various ways take on therapeutic roles (Lefley, 1987b).

Encountering the Mental Health System

Having a mentally ill person in the family means that it will be inexorably intertwined with the mental health system for an indefinite future. Professionals who have long been in the system may not appreciate what a new and bewildering world it is for those seeking help for the first time. To begin with, this search for help is occurring during a time of crisis when confusion and anxiety are high. Families may first turn to their family physician or clergyman for advice, which may or may not be helpful. The only initial source of help to some families is the yellow pages of the telephone book. With this inauspicious beginning, it may take a long time until the family and their ill relative feel effective as consumers. The mental health system is another environmental challenge and the road to competence in the use of this system is a difficult one.

In the section that follows, we will identify some consumer perspectives on problems in encountering the mental health system. This is not meant as a criticism of those who work in the system, nor do we presume at this time to suggest system changes. It is an effort to provide understanding of one more dimension of the family's dilemma in coping.

The Provider–Family Relationship

Upon entering the mental health system, a triadic relationship between practitioner, family, and patient must somehow evolve. However, the precise role that each should play is nowhere clearly defined. Families may struggle for a long time to understand what is expected of them, and may change services frequently until some kind of satisfaction is attained. The Western tradition of the helping professions has been paternalistic, as we noted earlier, in that professionals defined what was good for the consumer and professionals dispensed what they determined was needed (Steinman & Traunstein, 1976). Many of us grew up with this concept of medicine and many families may be comfortable with these defined roles. Much power lay in the hands of professionals with this treatment style.

One of the most enigmatic and deeply frustrating issues families face is the limitation on their decision making power because of patients' rights laws. No matter how dysfunctional patients are or how distorted their thinking, they are allowed to make their own decisions about serious matters that impinge on others at home and in the community. To families it is a crazy system since it does not allow the physician to order treatment in the best interests of the patient. It is incomprehensible to them that a loved one can remain in a serious state of deterioration and that they can only stand by until the person commits acts of dangerousness.

Other legalities confound the doctor–patient–family relationship. Doctors must hold in confidence anything the patient does not want shared with the family. Families may find themselves in a position in which they have little or no information about the patients' diagnosis, prognosis, and treatments, but still must make consumer decisions about treatment and rehabilitation or even provide care at home. This apparent irrationality of the system confounds and dismays families.

Diversity of Theory and Practice

Credibility of the mental health system is severely strained by the excessive diversity of theory and practice within the field, all of which the professions apparently accept as legitimate. The consumer is perplexed as to whom to believe. The family, then, in search of help in a number of clinical settings could be easily told a number of different and even contradictory explanations of what went wrong: Mothers are cold and rejecting (Fromm-Reichmann, 1948); families create "double binds" by giving the ill person contradictory messages (Bateson, Jackson, Haley, & Weakland, 1956); parents are suffering "marital schism" and "marital skew" (Lidz, 1973); parents have peculiar communication patterns (Wynne, 1987); there are disturbed family hierarchical relationships in the family (Haley, 1980; Madanes, 1981); there is high expressed emotion in the family (Leff & Vaughn, 1985); and so forth. Families lose confidence; they believe professionals do not know what they are doing. What might be a highly controversial, but stimulating intellectual field to professionals, is a nightmare to consumers who must make decisions as to which kind of help to engage. The problem is complicated by the professional's inability or unwillingness to explain in clear, jargon-free language what they assume about a family's relationship to mental illness, and the nature of the treatment they are recommending, including its potential risks and benefits.

Families may have assumed that mental health treatment is well regulated and that consumers are protected by law. But regulation of the mental health profession is primarily a responsibility of the profession itself, which has not done its job. Regulation has not been vigorous and the consumer has not been well protected. Mental health professionals are not whistle blowers, Levine (1981) reminds us; they believe in live and let live. This story of a 58-year-old mother illustrates how a family consumer may unwittingly purchase a service that denigrates those it exists to help:

> I didn't foresee his weird approach. The doctor radiated self-assurance. I am fat. We were shown charts that explained the dangers of overeating. My son was told that on days he did not spend 7 hours looking for employment, I would gorge and over-eat. He would be "killing" his mother. My son's personal psychiatrist noticed his regression caused by stress and instructed him not to attend any more. (Hatfield, Fierstein, & Johnson, 1982, p. 35)

Families of the mentally ill must often rely on publicly supported services. This poses other consumer dilemmas. Publicly supported services often have a virtual monopoly over the provision of a given type of service and thereby limit the kinds of choices that consumers can make. If there is only one clinic in a catchment area or one psychosocial center available, clients either have to take what is offered or do without. High demand and low supply tend to increase the power of agencies to resist change (Meenaghan & Mascari, 1971). When the clients do not fit the services, they are seen as resisting treatment. In some agencies, families may find that what professionals are trained to do, or what they prefer to do, dictates program content more than clients' needs do. The growth of consumer pressures may eventually change that, but, at present, it may be difficult to find a good fit between patient needs and available programs.

Making Economic Decisions

Once they find their way into the mental health system, families soon learn that the economic burden for care is bound to be high. The fact that these illnesses may need treatment over many years or even decades soon drains the resources even of the affluent. When first faced with mental illness, many families seek out the most prestigious and expensive treatment centers assuming that they can make their relative well. Disillusionment with the system sets in when, after long and costly treatment, their relative is still highly symptomatic.

Families may delude themselves into believing that the provision of mental health services is a wholly selfless act; therefore, they may not question the practitioner's recommendation for treatment and the length of time it must go on. They forget that professionals necessarily have very real and legitimate interests in a good income for services rendered, convenient hours and locations for their practices, and maintenance of status in their professions. Professional organizations teach their members how to increase demand for services, market them, and compete for the once plentiful mental health dollar. In addition to their interest in helping people, professional service providers are businesses in need of markets, and they may manufacture needs in order to have something to treat. It is hard for families who feel that the only reality is that of their suffering relative to realize that many other hard economic realities prevail. Consumers must become sophisticated if they are to get full value for the dollars they spend.

The need for accountability in the provision of services becomes uppermost in the minds of families. At a minimum, services should be safe and effective, accessible to those who need them, and reasonably priced. Peer review, professional organizations, boards of examiners and licensure, and training institutions should all play a part in insuring that minimum standards are met. But the responsibility for quality assurance is disproportionally in the hands of providers, who have financial stakes in the outcome. Those who use and pay for services have little to say about quality and appropriateness. With the growth of the National Alliance for the Mentally Ill (NAMI), this may be changing.

Those families that have mental health benefits in their insurance policies may be puzzled and dismayed when they learn that mental illness does not have the same benefits as physical illness. High deductibles, co-payments, and lifetime ceilings reduce coverage and increase out-of-pocket costs. In addition, these policies fail to cover the long rehabilitative treatment these patients need. These minimal benefits are now being threatened by new developments throughout the medical insurance industry, which makes the future of benefits for the mentally ill still more uncertain. On the horizon are various forms of prepaid services, group practices, and employer self-insurance (Dauner, 1986).

For those with severe mental illnesses who depend upon medicaid for care and treatment, the picture is also clouded. Medicaid, unfortunately, has followed the lead of private insurance companies in limiting mental health benefits. Community Mental Health Centers (CMHCs) also need attention because they were created to serve the mentally ill in their communities. How well these clinics serve them probably varies considerably from place to place.

The cost of care and the efficient use of existing resources will never cease to be an issue for families. They face a great challenge in trying to understand how care is financed in this country and how they as consumers can get the most value for their money. They will become advocates for change in the way mental health care is financed.

Summary

The onset of mental illness in a member creates a host of new problems that require immediate decisions and action. Families are thrust into a situation in which they must quickly learn about mental illness and begin devising strategies for appropriately responding to the needs of the disturbed individual while at the same time balancing the needs of other family members. Reorganization and reintegration of the family becomes urgent so that all necessary roles are performed and the life of the family can continue. The way that the family achieves its new balance may vary considerably and will depend upon the composition of the family, the roles formerly played by the impaired person, the current stage of the family life cycle, and the economic and cultural backgrounds of the group. In addition to the household's adjustment, other new challenges come that are inherent to involvement with the mental health and social services systems. These are new and complex systems for families to master, which they have a great urgency to do quickly. All in all, families of the mentally ill are faced with adaptive challenges that are accompanied by nearly intolerable levels of anxiety and stress.

While some may feel that we have presented too bleak a picture, we believe that our description is accurate for most families. We do not believe these situations are hopeless, however, for families struggle valiantly to survive. Later chapters will discuss ways that mental health professionals can be helpful allies in this struggle.

CHAPTER 4

New Directions in Providing Help to Families

In the last two chapters we have identified a wide range of problems that families encounter when a member becomes mentally ill. While the majority of families struggle along on their own and do an amazing job of creating solutions to complex problems, some require substantial help from others, and most could have their burdens lightened with appropriate help. Recently, we have seen a significant growth of interest in devising better ways to help families cope more effectively.

In the process of creating new programs, providers should be mindful of the mistakes of the past. These have been discussed a great deal in the literature and need only be mentioned briefly here. Most common was the mistake of blaming families for either causing mental illness or for perpetuating it in a vulnerable relative. Families were thus treated as patients rather than partners in treatment. In addition, families were often ignored and given little information about their relative's illness, nor were they advised about community resources. There was little concern about the stresses on the rest of the family, which were sometimes aggravated by overworked or uncaring professionals. Many of those developing newer programs are quite aware of the failures of the past and are working conscientiously to avoid them.

Whether the evolution toward better attitudes and working relationships with families is yet complete, however, is questionable. The author (Hatfield, 1986) examined the language used by some recent writers and reported that, while the more blatantly negative attitudes of the past were not so apparent, there were ways of talking about families that were a matter of concern. The author noted a frequent confusion of fact and inference, whereby interpretations of family behavior and judgments about them were bandied about as though they were fact. When statements of belief or opinion are stated often enough, they become reified and accepted as fact. Such statements as the "family sabotaged his plan" and that "family is overprotective" are familiar to many workers in the field. These are interpretations, and only interpretations, of some very complex family behavior. That same behavior might be interpreted in a number of other ways by other observers. This suggests that it is quite possible, and even likely, that we are wrong in many of our inferences that we make. While one cannot avoid interpretation, one must hold all interpretations as tentative and continue to check them against observable behavior. Families are frequently hurt by wrong interpretations that are uncritically held by professionals.

The author (Hatfield, 1986) noted that the language of some professionals tended to stereotype families by placing them in either/or categories. The popular concept of expressed emotion (EE) illustrates this point well. All families are divided into one of two polarities—"high EE" or "low EE"—as though such characteristics do not occur along a continuum. Other common polarities are: "functional" versus "dysfunctional," "enmeshment" versus "disenmeshment," "normal" versus "pathological." The author commented that "these are static concepts that characterize poorly the dynamic, fluid character of human life. They label rather than describe" (p. 328). The author also pointed out that general semanticists warn us that how we talk and how we think about others determines how we act toward them.

Further concerns expressed in that article had to do with, not only the use of either/or polarities in describing families, but also the negative judgments that were so often implied. Even though most of the articles were written in the 1980s, words such as "acrimonious," "noxious," and "pernicious" were still being used to describe families. Although there was a tendency to talk about teamwork and collaboration in some articles, in those same articles the language of control appeared. Writers talked about "using" or "handling" families, of "requiring" or "insisting" that families do as the provider directed, and also used language that presumed that the professional always knew what was good for others.

We are in a period of transition in the way we view families and work with them. It is inevitable that some old attitudes and language still persist. Not all professionals have yet thoroughly questioned their training and the theories that color their perceptions and guide their practices.

Understanding and evaluating new approaches to families is difficult because we are rarely supplied with their underlying assumptions or the theoretical frameworks that provide direction. We hope to remedy this common failure by stating the principles that guide our work. In Chapter 1, we have argued for the importance of taking into consideration the social context into which new programs are being projected. We have agreed with Mechanic (1980) that

> In current psychiatric literature, it is impressive to note how many public programs that are promoted are unrealistic in terms of manpower, the existing state of psychiatric knowledge and organizational and community resources. All too often programs are advocated and encouraged without sufficient attention being given to their feasibility or their consequences for social and political goals outside the realm of mental health. (p. 79)

We have identified as the most salient social concerns: new definitions of mental illnesses as brain diseases qualitatively different and distinct from adjustment problems; changing attitudes toward parents of the mentally ill; the growth of consumer power; the emergence of fiscal restraint; and ambiguity regarding responsibility for care. We see these as clear trends at this time, and we remind ourselves that change is inevitable. Unless we develop systems within which continuous innovation, renewal, and rebirth can occur, today's creative ideas may become tomorrow's dogma.

Our second major concern is that programs be developed within a clear conceptual framework that is made explicit. The theoretical framework that underpins our approach to families is that of coping and adaptation. Simply put, we see families of the mentally ill very much as we see other families who cope with other catastrophic events in their lives. We interpret the behaviors of these families as efforts to master environmental challenges characterized by uniqueness, ambiguity, pervasiveness, and persistence of highly different and difficult behaviors. We assume that of most importance to the family is the phenomenal world, for this is reality to them. Professionals must find ways to empathically understand the worlds of families of the mentally ill, with all their complexities, confusion, anxiety, and pain.

Education and support are the two approaches to helping families that best fit our theoretical model.

Education

The function of education is to develop long-term, organized bodies of knowledge and generic problem-solving skills that will help the learner solve problems in their lives both in the present and future. The focus in education is on both the broad application of what is learned and its retention over time. While many families may need immediate information and advice for the sake of efficiency, they also need to develop a background of information and general problem-solving skills that will make it possible for them to solve problems independently for an indefinite future.

To clarify the concept of education for mental health professionals, we have drawn substantially from Guerney, Stollak, and Guerney (1971). These writers assert that the medical model of helping all people in need will never be met. They recommend abandoning the medical model and deliberately following the model developed by educators over the centuries. Although a great deal has been written about the imperfections of the medical model by such well-known practitioners as Haley, Szasz, and others, it still dominates the applied field, as can be seen through the persistence of terms and concepts having to to with "pathology," "diagnosis," and "therapy." The time has come, according to Guerney and co-workers, to abandon the medical model in both practice and conviction.

These writers say that significant conceptual shifts are required to move from a medical practitioner model to an educator practitioner model. The first shift must be away from the implicit assumption held by both professional and client that a healing process of some kind is taking place. Instead, practitioners must recognize that they are dealing with questions of social, moral, and personal values that must be clearly stated at the outset and opened to debate. They must also shift their thinking away from the individual and toward more programmatic planning aimed at teaching specific groups of people clearly identified sets of attitudes, concepts, and skills. Any kind of testing should not be used for the purpose of uncovering the degree of "pathology" or "psychodynamics," but rather for aiding clients in making their own decisions about the courses of instruction they wish to follow.

According to the educational model, as Guerney and co-workers point out, practitioners should first define a specific set of attitudes, skills, and concepts that are likely to meet the felt needs of a reasonably large group of people. Planning should be for a group with, of course, a good educator's awareness of individual differences. Courses should be publicized in ways that other adult education courses are publicized. The educational model provides for low cost help because it deals with groups rather than individuals, and it lends itself to the eventual production of preprogrammed aids to learning (Guerney et al., 1971).

Guerney and others indicate considerable concern about values as they are expressed in medical versus educational models. Medical practice, they explain, directs its efforts mainly in the direction of universally held values. Practicing psychologists act as if they, like the physician, are dealing with sickness, absolutes, or universals, and not with questions of values and morals that are greatly affected by the culture in which the individual and the psychologist grew up. Psychosocial behaviors are culture-bound and are best conceived in relative, not absolute, terms. An educational model allows one to more easily recognize a value judgment for what it is. It even allows one—in a free and open discussion—to strongly advocate certain values over others. Educators should make values explicit and defend their value judgments.

Using an educational model does not prohibit dealing with individuals. Tutoring, which has long been considered an acceptable educational procedure, can be included in the educational model. In this way, group processes can be supplemented by individual assistance (Guerney et al., 1971).

Because education does not presume "pathology" or "dysfunction," connotations that many individuals resist, it is a more acceptable, less stigmatized method of acquiring help. There is some secrecy and embarrassment about needing therapy but there is public acceptance of education as a means to improvement.

Education as a way to prepare people to effectively cope with life circumstances has a long and respected tradition in this country. Our forefathers thought education to be so important that schooling for children was provided as soon as a settlement became partially stable, and, as early as 1636, Harvard University was established in the colony of Massachusetts. Educational approaches have historically been used to solve many social problems. In more recent years the concept of health education has emerged, especially as it relates to chronic illnesses such as cancer, diabetes, heart disease, cystic fibrosis, Alzheimer's disease, and the like. It is to be expected then that there will be a growing interest in education for people with severe and chronic mental illnesses and their families.

One of the earlier models of practical help to families was reported by Pasamanick, Scarpetti, and Dinitz (1967), who set up

home-care programs in which nurses were made available to families on a 24-hour basis. These providers predicted that "when a
community mental health center emerges, it is safe to assume that
this function of 'educating' families will become a vital and integral
part of the worker's role" (p. 75). Twenty years later we are beginning to see community mental health centers taking on this educational function with patients and with families.

Good models of educational approaches are more abundant
for those who work with younger children. The TEACCH model in
North Carolina is a well-developed strategy for working with highly
disturbed children. Their emphasis, as reported by Schopler,
Mesibov, Shigley, and Bashford (1984), is on developing competen-
cies and coping skills; it is a practical approach in which professionals adapt strategies to fit a family's style of coping. They operate
under the assumption that families are the experts on their own
children and that clinicians should avoid a judgmental attitude. In
addition, there must be an awareness of all the demands on a
family—economic, social, and emotional.

There is a growing interest in approaches that emphasize the
strength of people and their environments. The emphasis is on
developing competence through facilitating the natural adaptive
capacities of people (Maluccio, 1981). Maluccio uses the term competence for that repertoire of skills, knowledge, and qualities that
enable people to interact favorably with their environment. The
task, notes Hirschowitz (1976), is to promote, learn, and teach
coping, unequivocally defined as education.

Cognitive functions are among the most important in the
adaptive process (Fleming, 1981). They involve the reception, storage, organization, and manipulation of information. Cognitive processes have instrumental value in determining emotional reactions. Maluccio (1981) also feels that there should be greater
emphasis on the cognitive in coping and problem solving. In his
opinion, the use of the intellect has not been fully exploited.

Howell (1973), a family physician, believes that the primary
goal of mental health professionals should be teaching. Much of
what professionals know, she insists, can be taught to lay persons
in such a way that they can solve their own problems competently.
Howell expresses faith in the strength and wisdom of families once
they are armed with knowledge and faith in their "capabilities for
competent, sensible, and healthy self-determination" (p. xii). She
believes that when too many agencies are involved, families feel
more helpless, dependent, and incompetent. She feels that families

should insist that experts share their knowledge and skills so that they can conduct their own affairs and can use paid professionals at their own convenience and on their own terms.

Krauss and Slavinsky (1982) believe that families of the psychiatrically disabled can benefit from educational services, and they recommend that services be made available through local boards of education, churches, or community mental health centers. In classes or seminars, issues of diagnosis, prognosis, medication, and behavior problems can be directly addressed. Families are free to take or leave the advice they get without the burden of accounting for their decisions. Krauss and Slavinsky recommend research and experimentation with educational models.

In Sections II and III of this book, we more fully develop the theme of education by first presenting information that families need to know and then by discussing the process of education, or the techniques by which we try to make learning more efficient.

Support

Once mental health workers understand the consequences to families of having one of their members become mentally ill, their need for support from professionals becomes readily apparent. However, "support" is a frequently used concept that is rarely defined. Hence, significant attention to its meaning and practice is long overdue. Winston, Pinsker, and McCullough (1986) recently reviewed considerable literature on support and reported that they found no definitions of supportive therapy, no debate about definitions, and little attention to the utility of various supportive techniques.

Supportive relationships are essential components of all education for families. In supportive relationships, we are there for people in need. We communicate an interest and liking for them and a desire to be helpful. We reflect empathy for the painful dilemmas that they face, we offer reassurance and hope, and we express confidence in the person's strength and competence to surmount the present problems.

In supportive relationships, feelings and emotions play a larger part than does cognition. People receiving support feel validated as human beings, stronger and more competent, and more hopeful about the future. Techniques for developing supportive relationships will be more fully developed in Chapter 13.

In the remainder of this chapter, we will discuss two relatively new concepts of helping families that seem compatible with an adaptation framework. They are called "family consultation" and "family psychoeducation."

Consultation

Although education may be the most efficient and effective way to prepare families to cope with mental illness over the long haul, education may meet less well the needs of families in crisis or those families who prefer a one-on-one type of relationship. Heretofore, a request for individual help meant the family was assigned a patient role with therapy recommended. Some practitioners have come to see this approach as counterproductive. This has led to the search for new approaches to families that are more collaborative in nature. "Family consultation," as described below, is one such promising approach.

Kanter (1985) uses the word "consulting" to describe a way of working with families that is collaborative in nature. "In my experience," Kanter writes, "most families have the desire and the capacity to assist the patient and greatly welcome a respectful consultative approach" (p. 22). Kanter credits Caplan's (1970) classic work *The Theory and Practice of Mental Health Consultation* for helping him define the relationship involved as one of "coordinate interdependence" in which each side gives to and takes from the other. Successful consultation requires a continual flow of information from the family, with professional and family working together to solve emerging problems.

According to the Kanter model, the patient should be treated separately and should not be invited to attend the family session. This approach allows the other family members to ventilate negative emotions and to strategize without being interrupted by the patient. Also, by doing so the consultant can avoid the frustrating role of mediator.

Consulting professionals, Kanter advises, should have expertise in treating the chronically mentally ill that includes academic study and direct clinical experience with these patients. Useful background experience can be gained in milieu settings such as half-way houses, hospital wards, and day-treatment centers. Such experience helps consultants appreciate the stresses families face.

Wynne, McDaniel, and Weber (1987) arrived at their concept of "family consultation" in a way similar to that of Kanter. They note that family therapy no longer adequately characterizes the concepts or activities of the field. Recently, clinical, political, and economic circumstances have emerged that suggest the need for alternatives to the role of family therapist. Wynne and others believe that when families first seek help they are not looking for therapy. Rather, these individuals want advice or counseling about a problem. They are trying to understand the nature of the problem and what they can do about it. During this stock-taking period, "family consultation" is more appropriate than "family therapy."

Central to consultation is an emphasis on establishing a collaborative role relationship as the framework for discussing and agreeing upon a plan of action. This approach leaves options open until a thought-out consensus about how to proceed has been reached.

Wynne and colleagues (1987) see "family consultation" as a special case of "systems consultation" in which the consultant is a participant in the consultative system. Sometimes consultation leads to recommendations of family therapy and in some cases it may discourage such an undertaking. Often the effort is toward enhancement of healthy functioning with a focus on resources rather than pathology. When a problem can be reframed as an issue within the family's competency to solve, the authors explain, it helps families regain confidence, morale, and energy.

Finally, Wynne and co-authors point out that traditional family therapy is not looked on favorably by health-care administrators. Present economic conditions call for time-limited, efficient, targeted solutions rather than traditional cures.

At a recent conference on family education, sponsored by the National Alliance for the Mentally Ill (NAMI), Terkelsen (1987a) presented his evolving model of the consultant role. In a way similar to Kanter (1985) and Wynne and colleagues (1987), Terkelsen sees the consultative model as an attractive alternative to family therapy, and like them he sees it as a collaborative model in which parity exists between consultant and consultee.

Terkelsen's depiction of the family consultant seems to be analogous to those of other consultative roles—financial planners, tax advisors, and lawyers, for example. The consultee basically sets the agenda by identifying the problems needing solution. Families seeking help with a mentally ill relative arrive at the consultant's door because they are facing some dilemmas that they have not been able to solve alone. The consultant has the expertise to give advice and information and to make sound recommendations. Families bring with them chosen family members, and they return for consultation as little or as much as they feel they need to. Just as families have lawyers to whom they return over long periods of time, so would families have their family consultants to whom they could return when baffling new problems with mental illness emerged.

Consultation and education are ideal supplements to each other. Through education, families develop the understandings they will need over time and the ability to solve many of their own problems at an affordable cost since education can take place in groups. When families have a problem that needs individual attention, if they already have a course in mental illness behind them, they can more easily profit from their consultations.

Psychoeducation

Although the word "psychoeducation" is used a great deal in literature on work with families, there seems to be little consistency in the way it is used. We found that the term was used in the literature for approaches to families that varied considerably from lecture series and support groups to family therapy; psychoeducation took place in the home, clinic, and/or hospital. Sometimes the patient was included and sometimes not. The length of family involvement varied from a few hours to a year or more. A survey of professionals[1] who frequently use the term revealed little commonality in usage or understanding.

Difficulties in understanding the concept of psychoeducation are compounded because no theoretical assumptions about families, how they experience mental illness in a member, and what makes them respond as they do has been presented. Although there is a generally accepted model, the "stress–diathesis model," for thinking about patient behavior (see Anderson, Reiss, & Hogarty, 1986, p. 101), no theoretical model for understanding families is provided. Because many leaders in the area of psychoeducation were, or are, family therapists, we must assume that psychoeducation has its roots in family therapy and probably in family systems theory. To what extent psychoeducation departs from family systems approaches has not been clarified. Still it seems that some practitioners in psychoeducation have moved substantially

[1] Those responding to the survey were Carol Anderson, Kayle Bernheim, Stephen Cole, Michael Goldstein, Joel Kanter, Harriet Lefley, Karen Snyder, Leroy Spaniol, Kenneth Terkelsen, and Anthony Zipple.

toward an educational model, and some psychoeducation models seem quite compatible with coping and adaptation theory.

Although little conceptual clarity has been provided at this time, we find Snyder's (1984) efforts at separating educational from psychoeducational models useful. Education models, Snyder explains, have their roots in health education, especially as health education is used to help people care for those chronically ill. Education takes place in classes, lecture halls, or workshops and uses such approaches as didactic presentations, readings, and generic problem solving. In addition to Snyder's description of education, we would add the importance of teaching for long-term retention and for transfer of what is learned in the workshop or class to the daily living situation. In education the one in charge is called "leader," "instructor," or "teacher" and the recipients are called "participants" or "adult learners."

Psychoeducation and education are similar in that they both tend to have preplanned programs that, however, are modified to meet the needs of individual participants. These approaches differ from consultative models because the latter do not have preplanned programs, but rather take up immediate issues that families bring to their attention. The basic range of content and skill seem quite similar in all three modalities.

As we have become more familiar with the work of leaders in the field of psychoeducation (e.g., Anderson et al., 1986; Falloon, Boyd, & McGill, 1984; Goldstein, 1981; McFarlane, 1983), we have discerned some troublesome areas of difference. In psychoeducation, there is often an assumption of deficit, namely, high expressed emotion. It is not clear in the literature what high EE is. Is it a symptom of deeper pathology or is it a characteristic well within the "normal" range, undesirable only because people with schizophrenia experience discomfort with it? Since psychoeducation uses some of the language of the medical model, for example, words such as "therapy," "treatment," and "diagnosis," one naturally assumes that high EE means something is wrong with the person that needs treatment. "Caution must be exercised," Bernheim and Lehman (1985) warn, "to avoid dressing up old, negative attitudes in new terms" (p. 39). This kind of concern is bound to continue until the field clarifies what psychoeducation is. Is it an educational model or a medical one? Perhaps it is neither and needs to create the concepts and language that will define it as a totally new approach.

The assumption in educational approaches is that the primary focus is the family, its stresses, and its needs. While no one doubts that people with schizophrenia suffer enormously, they are or should be treated by professionals. The family's role is to help each other deal with the emotional fallout and to alter the home environment to best balance the needs of all members. It is not the family's role to be a psychotherapeutic agent for their disabled member. Psychoeducational approaches make the welfare of the patient the central concern, and the burden of keeping the patient from relapsing is placed upon the shoulders of the families.

The well-being of other family members is secondary in psychoeducational approaches. Although these programs are designed foremost for the needs of patients, when measures of family satisfaction have been taken, families usually have claimed that they have benefited.

Psychoeducation is a relatively new concept that can be expected to evolve considerably in the next few years. For purposes of research and practice, its theoretical underpinnings should develop; for the sake of families, a more clear and consistent delineation of psychoeducation should emerge.

Summary

Changes during the past decade in the way we view mental illnesses, growth in understanding of the family dilemma in accommodating a mentally ill relative, and a recognition of the social constraints in providing services to families, require that we seek new directions in working with families. The primary thrust is away from defining families as patients toward seeing them as collaborators in treatment. We no longer see families solely in terms of their supportive and therapeutic roles with the patient, but have come to concern ourselves with the quality of life of all members.

Four approaches to providing help to families are appropriate to our present understanding: education, consultation, support, and psychoeducation. Education is primarily a cognitive approach that concerns itself with the long-term retention of knowledge and its application to a broad range of problems, and which is the focus of the rest of this volume. However, supportive relationships are also essential to all approaches to families, and thus will also be discussed further.

II

Curriculum Content for Educational Programs

CHAPTER 5

Understanding Mental Illness

Basic to developing competence in solving any human problem is to establish a foundation of relevant information and knowledge. Families of the mentally ill are avid to know all that they can about mental illness—its nature, causes, prognosis, and treatment. It is only with these kinds of understandings that they can relate to their relative appropriately and solve a myriad of problems that arise because of mental illness. Some families go to great lengths to master the most technical aspects of mental illness and its treatments. Traditionally, mental health professionals were reluctant to share information with families. Why this was so is not clear. Anderson, Reiss, and Hogarty (1986) speculate that it may be because so little was reliably known. Professionals also may not have trusted families to understand and apply the information correctly, or might have thought that they might become worried, discouraged, and upset.

Anderson and colleagues argue for providing a solid knowledge base of mental illness so that families can develop reasonable expectations and realistic hope, as well as enable them to understand their relative's limitations and plan realistically with professionals for both short-term and long-term goals. Bernheim and Lehman (1985) support this view and point out that the provision of information is the first step toward developing a cooperative, consumer-oriented partnership with the ill person and the family. Collaboration requires a parity in expertise and responsibility. Believing that families have a need and a right to be knowledgeable, several professionals have written books in which technical information has been made understandable to lay audiences. Three of the books most often recommended by family educators to families are: *The Broken Brain* (Andreasen, 1984), *Surviving*

Schizophrenia: A Family Manual (Torrey, 1983), and *Schizophrenia: Symptoms, Causes, Treatments* (Bernheim & Lewine, 1979).

As we have noted in Chapter 1, we are living in a period of profound change in the way we have come to understand mental illnesses. Andreasen (1984) states that these changes are of revolutionary proportions insofar as psychiatry is realigning itself with mainstream medicine. During the past 10 to 20 years, Andreasen explains, the neurosciences have produced an explosion of knowledge about how the brain works, and this has taught us that the severe mental illnesses are due to abnormalities in brain structure and brain chemistry. In her words,

> Psychiatry, like the prodigal son, has returned home to its place as a specialty within the field of medicine. It has become increasingly scientific and biological in its orientation. Psychiatry now recognizes that serious mental illnesses are *diseases* in the same sense that cancer or high blood pressure are diseases. Mental illnesses are diseases that affect the brain, which is an organ of the body just as the heart or stomach is. (p. 8)

The biological model derives from Kraepelin and other neurologists of the late 19th and early 20th centuries, and, Andreasen says, even goes back to the time of classical Greece. In more recent times the biological model has been shaped by the neurosciences. The neurosciences work toward understanding the relationship between brain structure and function, and human thoughts, feelings, and behavior. Basic tenets of the biological model, selected from Andreasen (pp. 29–33, italics in original), are:

1. *The major psychiatric illnesses are diseases.* They should be considered medical illnesses just as diabetes, heart disease, and cancer are.
2. *These diseases are caused principally by biological factors, and most of these factors reside in the brain.* The brain is the organ of the body that monitors and controls the rest of bodily functions and is the source and storehouse of all psychological functions such as thoughts, memories, and feelings.
3. *The treatment of these diseases emphasizes the use of "somatic therapies."*
4. *Mental illnesses are not caused by weak character or bad parenting.*

Families of the mentally ill are eager to understand how brain functioning relates to their ill relative's troubling behavior. In addition, they are interested in questions of etiology, treatment, and long-term prognosis. Family educators find that families most often are dealing with diagnoses of schizophrenia, mood disorder, borderline personality disorder, or severe anxiety disorder. While the literature on each of these disorders is extensive, we have presented here a selected body of information that most families probably need.

Schizophrenia

Schizophrenia is a complicated and crippling disorder which impinges on all aspects of a person's life. The disorder tends to be chronic and episodic, and few people with the disease return to their premorbid state. Approximately 30% of hospital beds are occupied by patients with schizophrenia. Hence, the economic, social, and personal costs are astronomical. At the present time, there are no cures for schizophrenia, although there are treatments that can significantly improve functioning (Andreasen, 1984).

At the present time there are no known medical or psychological tests that can reliably confirm a diagnosis of schizophrenia. The disorder is inferred from the observation of behavior and from responses to treatment (Bernheim & Lewine, 1979). Questions naturally arise as to how reliably schizophrenia can be diagnosed. Bernheim and Lewine drew upon a study sponsored by the World Health Organization, which found that schizophrenia is diagnosed quite similarly in nine geographically and culturally different areas of the world, to affirm a fairly high degree of reliability. In each of these countries people with schizophrenia were characterized by similar symptoms: They lacked insight, were suspicious, held false ideas, suffered auditory hallucinations, and experienced passivity and emotional dullness. Bernheim and Lewine define schizophrenia as "a chronic disorder in which thinking, feeling, and relating tend to be disturbed in a characteristic way" (p. 8).

The process of thinking in a schizophrenic is usually disorganized and confused, resulting in bizarre communication and faulty judgment. Delusional thinking, defined as "fixed false beliefs," is common. Most often these delusions involve feelings of persecution and include suspiciousness, guardedness, and anger. The world becomes a terrifying place as the delusional individual experiences thoughts being inserted into her or his head, being broadcast, or being controlled by outside forces. Sometimes people with schizophrenia have delusions of grandeur in which they believe they have special missions in life (Andreasen, 1984; Anderson et al., 1986; Bernheim & Lewine, 1979). Families are astounded by the irrationality of these beliefs and learn with great frustration that they are quite unshakeable.

People with schizophrenia also frequently suffer various kinds of hallucinations. Hallucinations are abnormal perceptions such as hearing voices, seeing visions, or experiencing unusual bodily sensations. Auditory hallucinations are the most common. These voices can be very distressing, commenting on what the person is doing, or making mocking or derisive remarks (Andreasen, 1984).

While delusions and hallucinations are the best known symptoms of schizophrenia, they are not essential to schizophrenia. Torrey (1983) notes that there is no *single* symptom that is essential to a diagnosis of schizophrenia. Some patients have other combinations of symptoms, such as other kinds of thought disorder, disturbed affect, and disturbances of behavior without ever having delusions and hallucinations. "Most delusions and hallucinations," Torrey explains, "are a direct outgrowth of over-acuteness of the senses and the brain's inability to synthesize and respond appropriately to stimuli" (p. 23). These sensations are logical outgrowths of what the brain is experiencing, and seem logical and coherent to the person having them.

The behavior of people with schizophrenia is often unpredictable and incomprehensible. This regressed and bizarre behavior produces tremendous problems for patients and their families. Patients may be highly anxious and afraid and withdraw to their own inner world for safety. Emotions often seem dull or inappropriate to the situation. Hence, relationships with others invariably become impaired, leaving people with schizophrenia often leading lonely and isolated lives.

Anderson and colleagues (1986) go to some lengths to dispel the myths about schizophrenia. In their opinion, schizophrenia is not secondary to social labeling, nor is it a rational response to an irrational environment. Neither is it simply a failure in problem solving nor the result of early parenting. These writers say rather that *"schizophrenia is an environmentally sensitive and too often persistent or recurrent thought disorder with a rather convincing substrate of cerebral dysfunctioning* (cognitive, perceptual, anatomical, or biochemical) *that has been acquired* (via trauma, infection, etc.) *and/or inherited through one's genes"* (p. 5, italics in original). The organ of impairment is the brain.

Typically, schizophrenic patients simply do not adequately process stimuli or information from their environments. They have extraordinary difficulties, note Anderson and colleagues, in:

- Selecting relevant stimuli.
- Directing and maintaining attention.
- Recognizing and identifying stimuli.
- Integrating, storing, recalling, and using information appropriately.

People with schizophrenia are slow to process stimuli even under predictable conditions; they have even more difficulty when there is competing information. This leads them to a sense of being overwhelmed with stimuli and unable to attend to what is most relevant.

A number of current writers in the field of psychoeducation use a stress–diathesis model to explain mental illness (Anderson et al., 1986; Bernheim & Lewine, 1979; Falloon, Boyd, & McGill, 1984). Bernheim and Lewine say schizophrenia occurs as the result of three factors: internal physiology, psychological predisposition, and environmental stress. The "diathesis" refers to the biochemical predispositions that must be present in order for the illness to manifest itself, and "stress" refers to the environmental occurrences to which the individual is reacting.

Biological Explanations

Schizophrenia is probably a group of brain diseases in which there are both structural differences and functional differences between normal brains and those with schizophrenia. The limbic system of the brain is now thought to be the site of many of the problems associated with schizophrenia. Although the limbic system is very small, it has direct connections to all major parts of the brain, and the system contains most of the elements that define individual personality, cognitive style, and patterns of behavior. Many brain scientists maintain the basic expectation that the key to understanding many aspects of mental illness may lie within the limbic system and its connections. No specific defect in the limbic system has been uncovered yet, but a clustering of evidence and the effect of drug treatments suggest that this may be so (Andreasen, 1984; Torrey, 1983).

Many scientists now also believe that a part of the explanation for schizophrenia lies in the way neurotransmitters function in the brain. Many neurotransmitters are concentrated in the limbic system, hence, their malfunction might have significant influences on the limbic system. Electrical impulses flow down the axons of neurotransmitters to hundreds of nerve terminals that communicate with other neurons. These communication points are referred to as a "synapses." Communication across these synapses is accomplished by biochemical means. It appears that mental illness is due to a breakdown in neurotransmitter systems due to chemical imbalances. Thus, treatment involves correcting these imbalances (Andreasen, 1984).

Dopamine is the neurotransmitter that is thought to be excessively elevated in some patients suffering from schizophrenia. Many drugs used to treat schizophrenia decrease dopamine transmission. The dopamine system is located in the midbrain, the substantia nigra, and the hypothalamus. Dopamine-containing cells of the midbrain project to the limbic system, which may be the seat of disturbance in schizophrenia (Andreasen, 1984).

Other brain abnormalities have also been observed in people with schizophrenia. One of these has to do with the ventricular system, which consists of four fluid-filled cavities lying deep within the brain. When brain cells are damaged or die, the substance of the brain grows smaller and the ventricles enlarge to fill empty spaces within the skull (Andreasen, 1984). Patients having these abnormalities are more likely to have severe symptoms of withdrawal and flattening of affect and are less likely to respond to medications (Torrey, 1983).

Thus, notes Torrey, both the structure and function of schizophrenic brains have been shown to be different. In fact, it is no longer useful to distinguish between the two since all explanations now lie in the organic.

Causes

There is no known single cause of schizophrenia. It appears that genetic factors produce a vulnerability to schizophrenia, with environmental factors contributing to different degrees in different individuals. It has long been known that schizophrenia runs in families. Children of a schizophrenic parent, for example, have about a 10% chance of developing schizophrenia. Recent studies of identical twins have supported earlier less scientific studies. An important group of studies was conducted in Denmark of adopted-away children of schizophrenic parents. These children were compared to adopted children whose parents had no history of schizophrenia. Findings of these studies indicate that being biologically related to a schizophrenic person increases the risk for schizophrenia, even when the related individuals have had little or no contact (Shore, 1986).

Genetic factors are important but not enough so to make up the total explanation. What, then, are plausible environmental explanations? One hypothesis is that schizophrenia may be due to a viral illness occurring early in life that produces some kind of brain inflammation that predisposes people to the development of the disease. This hypothesis has been supported in part by the identification of virus-like agents in the spinal fluid of people having schizophrenia and by the excess of schizophrenics having winter births, a time when viral illnesses occur with a particular frequency. Some evidence suggests that patients suffering from schizophrenia may be more likely to have mild or "soft" signs of brain damage occurring early in life (Andreasen, 1984). Most schizophrenia researchers now agree that parents do not cause schizophrenia in their offspring (Andreasen, 1984; Shore, 1986; Torrey, 1983).

Prognosis

Families are deeply concerned about what the future holds for their mentally ill relatives. Although no cures have yet been found, families can be given hope that a fairly independent and satisfying life for people with schizophrenia is possible. With time and active collaboration between patient, family, and doctor, many of the most disabling symptoms of the illness can be managed with the use of neuroleptic medication. Also, there is an increasing variety of rehabilitation services available in most communities to help patients learn—or relearn—social and vocational skills.

Harding, Zubin, and Strauss (1987), in a recent provocative article, challenge the prevailing view of the chronic course of schizophrenia. They reviewed the literature on long-term outcome of a schizophrenic illness and report many methodological flaws. In their view, there is wide variation in the courses of the illness. With symptoms changing over time, no one can currently predict who will get better or how many people will actually get well and leave the mental health system altogether.

Major Mood Disorders

Mood disorders are the most common psychiatric disorders. They include two major groups of illness: bipolar or manic–depressive disorders, and major depressive disorders. As their name indicates, mood disorders are characterized primarily by a disturbance in affect. People so afflicted experience uncontrollable extremes of either elation or sadness. Serious depression affects 5% of the population at any point in time, and, at least 10% of people will suffer a severe depression at some point in their lives (Andreasen, 1984; Greist & Jefferson, 1984; Kline, 1974).

The person who is depressed feels sad, despondent, blue, and full of despair and hopelessness. There may be complaints about poor concentration, poor memory, and difficulty with making decisions, as well as exaggerated fears about certain situations. There are generally pessimistic attitudes about the present and the future (Greist & Jefferson, 1984).

Patients with severe depression may experience appetite disturbances (either eating too much or too little), sleep disturbances (usually difficulty falling asleep or awakening early in the morning), fatigue, and loss of interest in usual things, including sex (Greist & Jefferson, 1984). Depressed patients may feel guilty over actual or imagined misdeeds. Some patients become preoccupied with death and begin to consider suicide—the most serious complication of depression. Approximately 15% of all hospitalized patients suffering from depression eventually commit suicide (Andreasen, 1984).

The most severe depressions may be accompanied by hallucinations and delusions and may be referred to as psychotic depressions. These usually occur only when the mood is highly disturbed and usually disappear when moods return to normal. This differentiates them from schizophrenia, in which delusions and hallucinations tend to be fairly constant (Andreasen, 1984).

About 10% of people with depression will also experience mania, and they are said to have manic–depressive or bipolar disorder. During mania, moods swing to an elevated, expansive, elated, or even euphoric state. The person may sleep very little, talk excessively and rapidly, eat very little, and feel like her or his thoughts are racing. Sometimes poorly considered decisions are made that result in serious consequences for the individual (Andreasen, 1984; Kline, 1974).

"The person with manic depression," notes Andreasen, "is pathologically happy" (p. 45). It is hard to say a person "suffers" from mania, she says, for such people seem to have boundless enthusiasm and good will. Many of them refuse to recognize that they have a problem. People who are suffering from mania may be unusually active, their sexual behavior may be inappropriate, they may be excessively social and gregarious—going to bars, planning parties, and calling up friends all hours of the day and night (Andreasen, 1984).

Friends and relatives may first note the onset of mania by changes occurring in the way the person talks. Speech seems to be pressured, sentences may go unfinished, and the amount of talking may become excessive. There is a quality of verbosity that exhausts others. Attention is sometimes drawn to persons with mania because they get into trouble with their tendencies to judge poorly and be full of grandiosity (Andreasen, 1984; Kline, 1974).

Typically manic–depressive conditions are cyclical in nature. The onset of high and low periods seems to be quite independent of other circumstances in the patient's life. For some patients, highs and lows can be quite accurately predicted on the basis of their cyclic history.

Neurochemical Factors

It is now generally believed that mood disorders are due to chemical imbalances in the brain. The "catecholamine hypothesis" about mood disorders says that depression may be due to a deficiency of norepinephrine whereas mania may be due to an excess of it. Norepinephrine is one of the major catecholamine systems in the body. The catecholamines are very active in the peripheral nervous system, the part outside of the brain that governs bodily functions such as heart rate and blood pressure (Andreasen, 1984).

The catecholamine hypothesis has been supplemented by the "serotonin hypothesis." Serotonin is another major transmitter in the central nervous system. Unlike dopamine, which is fairly well localized in specific areas, serotonin and norepinephrine are present in nerve endings located in many parts of the brain (Andreasen, 1984).

In addition to the two explanations of mood disorders just described, there may be a third type related to endocrine function. Imbalance may be due to improper regulation of the endocrine system through secretions that arise in the hypothalamus and pass on to the pituitary gland. The pituitary sends out hormones, or chemical messengers, that are circulated through the blood to target such organs as the thyroid, the adrenal glands, and the ovaries. Abnormalities appear not to lie in these organs, but rather in the hypothalamus or at some other location not yet established (Andreasen, 1984).

Etiological Factors

Family studies have consistently shown that relatives of people suffering from mood disorders have a much higher rate of mania and depression than found in the general population. The fact that relatives of people with bipolar disorder have both bipolar and unipolar disorder, as do the relatives of patients who have depression only, suggest that mania and depression may not be different disorders but rather may be the same illness with different degrees of severity (Andreasen, 1984). Andreasen suggests that bipolar illness may be a more severe form of depressive disorder.

In family studies it has been reported that about 20% of the parents of patients with mood disorders also have mood disorders, while the rate for siblings is even higher—possibly as high as 30%, although the rate tends to be higher for sisters than brothers. Twin and adoptive studies have also been done for mood disorders. The concordance rate for identical twins is 50–60% (Andreasen, 1984).

The environment or social factors that trigger the onset of an affective illness may be either physical or psychological. Physical influences may vary considerably from major ones such as a heart attack to minor ones such as a cold. Social factors can be acute stressors, such as an accident or loss of job, or such long-term stressors as coping with an incompatible marriage or caring for an elderly parent or a chronically ill child.

Prognosis

Although depressive illnesses spare no segment of the population and cause immense suffering, they are quite treatable. The prospects for recovery are not related to the depth of the depression. Very severe cases often respond well to treatment whereas an occasional mild case may prove resistant to treatment. The decisive factor is the individual patient's response to the drugs being given (Kline, 1974). Treatments for depression will be discussed further in Chapter 7.

Depressed people and those around them must be aware of the risk of suicide. In terms of predicting suicide, it is important to know that risk of suicide climbs steadily with age up to the age of 70. Those over 65 make up 11% of the population but account for

25% of all suicides. Also, males are three or four times more likely to die of suicide; 60% of those who kill themselves have made a previous attempt; and finally, a recent loss and social isolation are associated with suicide (Greist & Jefferson, 1984).

Other Major Disorders

In working with families of mentally ill people, professionals will find the most common diagnoses to be schizophrenia and mood disorders. There may be others, however, of which the most likely are borderline personality disorder and anxiety disorder.

Borderline Personality Disorder

Borderline personality disorder has historically been a subject of much confusion and controversy. There appears to be agreement, however, that there is an identifiable borderline syndrome; that is, that there is a cluster of characteristics that occur together with greater than chance frequency and that differentiates the patient from other patient groups (Gunderson, 1984). This disorder was once closely linked with the schizophrenic spectrum, but this is no longer the case. The support for linkage to mood disorders, although not conclusive, is more widely accepted (Davis & Akiskal, 1986; Gunderson, 1984). Gunderson believes that the treatment problems posed by borderline patients are sufficiently unique that the development of a distinct psychiatric diagnosis is warranted.

People with borderline personality disorder, according to Maxmen (1986), feel chronically bored and empty and are in desperate search of stimulation. They might gamble, sexually act-up, abuse drugs, overdose, instigate brawls, or attempt suicide. Their moods are always reactive, intense, and brief. Borderlines have seriously disturbed interpersonal relationships. People with this disorder hate being alone, are intensely dependent on others, and become exceedingly angry if others do not fill their needs. They tend to see people in black and white, never gray, and they start by idealizing others and wind up devaluing them. Borderline personality disordered people have a unique capacity for creating dissension between other people (Maxmen, 1985). Others find borderlines exhausting.

People with borderline personality may be physically self-damaging; for example, they may make suicidal gestures, mutilate themselves, or get into frequent accidents or physical fights. They

may become psychotic for brief periods of time. People with borderline personality present considerable treatment difficulties.
Long-term psychotherapy is usually recommended although no
well-done studies at this time support the efficacy of this approach.
Low doses of antipsychotic and/or antidepressant medication are
sometimes used (Maxmen, 1985).

Borderline personality disorder tends to run in families. When
compared with controls, first-degree relatives have this disorder at
a rate ten times greater and are three times more likely to be
alcoholics. Relatives also have higher rates of depressive disorder
but normal rates of schizophrenia and bipolar disorder.

Anxiety Disorders

Anxiety should only be considered pathological, and therefore a
symptom of psychiatric disorder, when it ceases to be adaptive and
instead becomes crippling and disabling. Anxiety disorders are
characterized by a mixture of physical and psychological symptoms, but doctors do not agree about the relative importance of
each or which might be underlying factors. Typical physical symptoms are a pounding heart, a rapid pulse, chest pain or tightness,
sweating, nausea, dizziness, weakness, and fatigue. The psychological symptoms include tension, nervousness, apprehensiveness,
hyperalertness, and subjective feelings of terror or panic (Andreasen, 1984).

Anxiety disorders are usually divided into three main groups:
phobic disorders, anxiety states, and post-traumatic stress syndrome. Agoraphobia is probably the most common and most crippling of phobic disorders. Those with this disorder have a fear of
being alone or in public places from which they may be unable to
escape. Typical objects of fear are tunnels, bridges, and elevators.
Patients with agoraphobia may increasingly restrict their activity
until they are virtually housebound. Social and simple phobias
involve more circumscribed stimuli. Social phobia is a fear of
situations in which the person may be subjected to scrutiny by
others. Common social phobias include fear of eating in restau-
rants, fear of public speaking, or fear of using public lavatories.
Simple phobias include all other phobias, such as fear of animals or
fear of heights (Andreasen, 1984).

Phobic disorders all involve fear of some specific stimulus
such as heights, crowds, or animals. In anxiety states, the anxiety is
not tied to a specific stimulus but tends to be more generalized.
One form of anxiety illness is panic disorder in which an attack

involves the sudden onset of pounding heart, chest pains, dizziness, shortness of breath, and feelings of impending doom. These attacks usually last only a few minutes although occasionally they may last longer. A second form of anxiety illness is generalized anxiety in which there is a persistent, pervasive anxiety. A third form that an anxiety illness may take is obsessive–compulsive disorder. An obsession is a persistent troubling thought that the person recognizes as senseless but is unable to get rid of. A compulsion is a senseless repetitive act, such as handwashing, counting, or touching. These disorders are difficult to treat (Andreasen, 1984).

Post-traumatic stress syndrome has gotten much attention since the Vietnam War. It occurs after participating in combat, but may also be an aftermath of the holocaust, airplane crashes, or earthquakes. People who have these traumatic experiences typically relive them in a variety of ways. They may experience sleep difficulty, loss of interest in life, and loss of ability to feel (Andreasen, 1984).

Our understanding of the anxiety disorders seems to lie in the gamma-aminobutyric acid (GABA) system of the brain. Investigators believe that the GABA system has an inhibitory effect and that anti-anxiety drugs work to enhance this effect and slow down other brain systems. Work in the neurochemistry of anxiety is too new to have produced a well-developed explanation, but it does appear that the brain contains mechanisms to regulate psychological states such as anxiety (Andreasen, 1984). Evidence is slowly accumulating that a predisposition to anxiety disorders may be partly hereditary.

Summary

In this chapter we have summarized some of the essential information that families will need to know in order to be an effective support system to a mentally ill member. New investigations are going on all the time, however, so much of this may change. Those who take on the task of teaching families this information must keep abreast of new developments so families can receive accurate and up-to-date information. Instructors can identify written materials, lectures, classes, etc., that will enable families to continue their quest for scientific knowledge on their own.

CHAPTER 6

The Personal Side
of Mental Illness

Families are bewildered, frustrated, and sometimes terrified by the irrational behavior and bizarre language of a mentally ill relative. Knowing that the behavior is due to a brain dysfunction is of considerable importance to these families in learning to cope successfully. In addition, however, an empathic understanding of their relative's experience in living with these strange disorders is necessary.

Torrey (1983) makes an eloquent plea for the necessity of families to understand the "inner world of madness," for, when tragedy strikes, he explains, one of the things that makes life bearable is the sympathy of friends and relatives. The "prerequisite for sympathy is an ability to put oneself in the place of the person afflicted" (p. 5). Sympathy for those afflicted with mental illness is sparse because it is so difficult to understand what lies behind the strange language and bizarre behavior. When people develop mental illnesses they no longer seem to be the same. It is as though another personality has taken over the loved one. Nevertheless, as Torrey insists in the case of schizophrenia, it is the obligation of everyone with a close friend or relative with the illness to learn as much as possible about the disease and what the afflicted person is experiencing. He states:

> With sympathy, schizophrenia is a personal tragedy. Without sympathy, it becomes a family calamity, for there is nothing to knit people together, no balm for the wounds. Understanding schizophrenia helps to demystify the disease and brings it from the realm of the occult to the daylight of reason. As we come to

understand it, the face of madness slowly changes before us
from one of terror to one of sadness. For the sufferer, this is a
significant change. (Torrey, 1983, p. 6)

Those who have suffered from these illnesses have expressed
their displeasure at being only objects of treatment and not fully
understood. McGrath (1984), in reaction to the technological explanations of brain disease, says:

I suddenly feel that my humanity has been sacrificed to a com-
puter printout, that the researchers have dissected me without
realizing that I am still alive. I am not comfortable or safe in all
their certain uncertainties—I feel they are losing me, the person,
more and more. (p. 639)

Brundage (1983) recalls her recovery from mental illness and
concludes:

The effectiveness in reaching and working with patients rests
largely upon the ability of the caregiver to perceive and comprehend how particular patients are experiencing their illnesses. . . .
Feedback that is understandable to patients in their world is the
essence of helpfulness. (p. 585)

In the 1960s there were a number of attempts to bring together first-person accounts of people suffering from mental illness (e.g., Alvarez, 1961; Kaplan, 1964; Landis & Mettler, 1964).
Kaplan insists that there is no better starting point for those seeking understanding of baffling mental disorders than personal accounts with the experience, for here we come into intimate contact
with the reality of mental illness itself. Kaplan believes that often
psychiatry has not listened carefully enough to its patients, choos-
ing instead to take seriously only what it could observe and verify.
In their zeal for the hard stuff of science, psychiatrists sometimes
reject the patient experiences as subjective, impressionistic, liable
to distortion, and impossible to verify. Those of a Freudian persuasion assume that the patient's experience is one of self-deception
and that its reality is hidden from her or him.

Kaplan cautions that the patient's account of her or his experience should not be taken for the experience itself. The latter
tends to have an ineffable quality difficult for ordinary language to
communicate. In addition, there is always some selectivity and
distortion, and some forgetting is inevitable. At best we have faulty

reconstructions of what was actually experienced. Nevertheless, the patient *knows* what the outsider can only infer.

In more recent years, Carpenter (1986) and Strauss (1986) have emphasized the importance of understanding the phenomenological side of mental illness. Carpenter says:

> The most irreducible essence of our interest in schizophrenia is the nature of another person's experience. It is in the subjective and inner world of volition, perception, cognition, and affect that schizophrenia is manifest. Empathy is crucial in discovering the subjective life of another person, and to engage in this process with a psychotic person, requires skill, intuition, and perseverance. (p. 534)

Strauss (1986) emphasizes the importance of understanding the personal side of schizophrenia in the field of psychiatric rehabilitation. There is growing evidence, he states, that the individual characteristics of a person will help determine part of the course and outcome of schizophrenia. Important to understand are the efforts the person makes in her or his own behalf, the role of meanings, and the sense of identity that the person has.

Schizophrenia is a terrifying disease for both the clinician and the patient. As Minkoff and Stern (1985) point out, "The devastation, shame, and despair of the experience of chronic psychosis makes empathy very painful for even the most experienced clinician, let alone the trainee" (p. 863). Not only is it difficult to connect with the patient behind the bizarre symptomatology, once the connection is made, the patient's despair at being chronic may be more than the clinician can tolerate.

To understand this inner world of mental illness, we will rely heavily on the way that patients describe their experiences, as well as summaries of patient experiences prepared by other writers.

Experiencing Mental Illness

The works of several authors were heavily relied upon for this section of the chapter. The work of Freedman (1974), in which he synthesized over 50 autobiographical books and articles, was especially useful, as were the works of Torrey (1983), Anscombe (1987), and Kaplan (1964). In addition, some more recent first-person accounts by patients and former patients provide valuable insights.

Altered Perceptions

Alterations of senses may involve either enhancement or blunting of the senses, but enhancement or increased acuteness is most common. Things become more vivid, acute, and intense. Visual stimuli appear sharper and brighter and auditory stimuli louder and more distinct. Torrey (1983) provides the following example from a patient:

> During the last while back I have noticed that noises all seem to be louder to me than they were before. It is as if someone had turned up the volume. . . . I noticed it most with background noises—you know what I mean, noises that are always around but you don't notice them. Now they seem to be just as loud and sometimes louder than the main noises that are going on. . . . It's a bit alarming at times because it makes it difficult to keep your mind on something when there's so much going on that you can't help listening to it. (pp. 7–8)

People with schizophrenia also find themselves staring at things; they describe this as their attention being captured by incidental aspects of their environment. Minor details of color, texture, or form capture the patient's attention and they retain an importance that is out of proportion to their true significance (Anscombe, 1987, p. 247). A former patient provides the following experience:

> I seem to be noticing colors more than before, although I am not artistically minded. The colors of things seem much . . . clearer and yet at the same time there is something missing. The things I look at seem to be flatter as if [I] were looking just at a surface. (McGhie & Chapman, 1961, p. 105)

A patient's perception may jam so that she or he remains stuck on a single thought or perception. The patient is not able to maintain control over the way she or he holds or shifts attention. Attention is captured by incidental details. Anscombe (1987), quoting from Sechehaye (1970), illustrates this point:

> As soon as my gaze fell on a spot of any sort, a shadow, or a ray of light, I could not drag it away, caught and held fast by the boundless world of the infinitely small. To wrench myself out of this impasse I began to beat on the table or on the wall with both fists. (p. 248)

Sometimes there is misperception or distortion of a genuine external stimulus. Once familiar sights may appear different from the way the patient remembered them, or they may change before her or his eyes (Freedman, 1974). Sechehaye (1964) illustrates this phenomenon:

> I saw things, smooth as metal, so cut off, so detached from each other, so illuminated and tense that they filled me with terror. When, for example, I looked at a chair or a jug, I thought not of their use or function—a jug not as something to hold water or milk, a chair not as something to sit on—but as having lost their name, their functions, and their meanings; they became "things" and began to take on life, to exist. (p. 169)

Another example occurs in a newsletter of a local chapter of the National Alliance for the Mentally Ill (NAMI):

> It is hard to describe what real psychosis is because when you are in it, it's hard to be clear. The world seems underwater, and my nervous system on the outside, buffeted by mental winds, blinking lights and dog barks that might as well be guns and tanks from my pain and fear. (Sharp, 1987, p. 1)

Torrey (1983) has noted that some patients' comments indicate that they have great difficulty synthesizing incoming stimuli. He illustrates the point with the following two examples:

> I have to put things together in my head. If I look at my watch I see the watch strap, face, hands and so on, then I have to put them together to get it into one piece. (p. 15)

> If I do something like going for a drink of water, I've got to go over each detail—find cup, walk over, turn tap on, fill cup, turn tap off, drink it. I keep building up a picture. I have to change the picture each time. I've got to make the old picture move. I can't concentrate. I can't hold things. Something else comes in, various things. It's easier if I stay still. (p. 17)

Torrey (1983) also finds that some patients are unable to synthesize auditory and visual stimuli into a coherent pattern.

> I can't concentrate on television because I can't watch the screen and listen to what is being said at the same time. I can't seem to take in two things like this at the same time especially when one

of them means watching and the other means listening. On the other hand I seem to be always taking in too much at one time and then I can't handle it and can't make sense out of it. (p. 15)

People with schizophrenia often have difficulty filtering out irrelevant stimuli and feel overloaded with it. "What happened to me in Toronto," one patient related, "was a breakdown in the filter, and a hodge-podge of unrelated stimuli were distracting me from things which should have had my undivided attention" (MacDonald, 1960, p. 218). Torrey (1983) says that it is as if the brain were being bombarded by stimuli, both internal and external, and the mind flooded with thought. One of his patients had the following to say about this phenomenon:

My trouble is that I've got too many thoughts. You might think about something, let's say that ashtray, and just think, oh! yes! that's for putting my cigarette in, but I would think of it and then I would think of different things connected with it at the same time. (p. 10)

Sometimes the person has the sensation that someone is inserting thoughts into her or his head, as in the following:

All sorts of "thoughts" seem to come to me, as if someone is "speaking" them inside my head. When in any company it appears to be worse (probably some form of self-consciousness), I don't want the "thoughts" to come but I keep "hearing" them (as it were) and it requires a lot of will power sometimes to stop myself from "thinking" (in the form of "words") the most absurd and embarrassing things. (Torrey, 1983, p. 11)

Difficult to understand by professionals and families alike is how seductive these unreal experiences can be for some of the patients who have them.

It is more real than reality. For nothing that happens to a sane mortal in the common-place world of ordinary living can approach the startling intensity of things going on in a delusion. There is a sharpness—a shrillness—a piercing intensity which thrusts itself through the consciousness and is so much more convincing than the blunt edge of reason, that even if the two are conflicting there is no choice between them. (Jefferson, 1964, p. 18)

Should I let anyone know that there are moments, just moments in schizophrenia that are "special"? When I feel that I am traveling to some place I can't go "normally"? Where there is an awareness, a different sort of vision allowed me? Moments that I can't make myself believe or just symptoms of craziness and nothing more. The time when colors appear brighter, alluring almost, and my attention is drawn into shadows, the lights, the intricate patterns of texture, the bold outlines of the objects around me. . . . and everything is wonder. (McGrath, 1984, p. 639)

In the quotation above, McGrath shows how his attention was *drawn* into the shadows, the lights, and patterns of texture. It was as though some force outside of himself controlled his attention and he was required to passively attend to what was there. This is a fairly common phenomenon reported by patients.

Attentional Deficits

Problems in focusing attention and concentrating are mentioned more often than any other cognitive or perceptual disorder in Freedman's sample of patients. Over half of his total sample specifically noted problems in concentrating on reading, writing, and speaking, or said that their minds wandered a good deal. Freedman (1974) illustrates this point with a quotation from a patient:

It is not that he (the patient) cannot keep to the point, but there are so many points and all equally and insistently insignificant, like a starlit sky with 50 different polestars in the sky. (p. 336)

Some patients report great susceptibility to distractions:

My concentration is poor. I jump from one thing to another. If I am talking to someone they only need to cross their legs or scratch their heads and I am distracted and forget what I was saying. I think I could concentrate better with my eyes shut. (Torrey, 1983, p. 10)

Some patients report feeling bombarded by stimuli making them unable to select out the relevant portion of the total input. Instead, the irrelevant parts impinge on them with as much salience as do the relevant. Some patients report that their inability to concentrate is impaired by the emergence of hallucinatory material into their thinking (Freedman, 1974).

Anscombe (1987) strongly emphasizes attentional deficit as being central to the schizophrenic experience. He notes a marked inability to sustain an intentional focus on attention. The patient has the sensation of being captured by a stimulus rather than being in control and able to choose what to pay attention to, and finds that she or he cannot shift her or his attention flexibly, not because something is important, but because attention does not shift easily. Sometimes a patient's attention may get stuck or blocked by something of little consequence. Anscombe uses the following patient report to point out this problem:

> If I am reading I may suddenly get bogged down at a word. It may be any word, even a simple word that I know well. When this happens I can't get past it. It is as if I am being hypnotized by it. It's as if I am seeing the word for the first time and in a different way from anyone else. It's not so much that I absorb it, it's more like it is absorbing me. (McGhie & Chapman, 1961, quoted in Anscombe, 1987, p. 247)

In schizophrenia, objects seem to jump out and command attention, even though this attraction may have little to do with what the person is really interested in. Finding themselves riveted to a particular stimulus, Anscombe says, makes people with schizophrenia conclude that what they are attracted to has unusual significance. Things appear significant because they have captured attention, and then the salience is interpreted to mean something. Patients feel impelled to react by making sense of it in some way. David Zelt (1981), who tells his story in the third person, describes his fascination with colors, each of which came to have their own significance:

> Ordinarily, unimportant information from external reality took on new dimensions for him. For example, colors powerfully influenced him. At any given moment wherever David went, colors were used to express judgments about his spirituality. People used the colors of their clothes or cars to express positive or negative views of him. Green meant that David was like Christ; white stood for his spiritual purity; orange indicated he was attuned to the cosmos. (p. 530)

The capturing of attention and the apparent role of external circumstances in assigning meaning leads to a variety of interpretations—telepathy, thought control, radio receivers, and electronic brain implants. Unable to direct their attention to long-term memory or other data that might help to correct and reassess what is being encountered, people with schizophrenia yield to distorted and delusional thinking.

Some patients give up the struggle to assert themselves since the self hardly exists that can impose its will on thought and action. They undergo experiences that hardly seem to be their own. McGhie and Chapman (1961) illustrate this phenomenon:

> Things just happen to me now and I have no control over them. I don't seem to have the same say in things anymore. At times, I can't even control what I want to think about. I am starting to feel pretty numb about everything because I am becoming an object and objects don't have feelings. (p. 109)

Given the amount of perceptual and attentional difficulties people with mental illnesses face, it is not surprising to find that significant cognitive confusion prevails.

Cognitive Confusion

Patients in Freedman's (1974) study frequently described themselves with words like confused, hazy, foggy, bewildered, and disoriented. Thought blocking was reported by several patients, who thought of it as their minds going blank, or experiencing a sudden loss of all thought.

The loosening of associations or disconnectedness in speech show the difficulty some patients have in tracking a particular idea. Sometimes the person starts a sentence or thought, but thinking veers off in another direction. The individual is unable to maintain cognitive control (Anscombe, 1987). Torrey (1983) provides an example of this:

> My thoughts get all jumbled up. I start thinking or talking about something but I never get there. Instead I wander off in the wrong direction and get caught up with all sorts of different things that may be connected with the things I want to say but in a way I can't explain. People listening to me get more lost than I do. (p. 18)

Another characteristic of schizophrenia is concrete thinking. People with the disorder have difficulty thinking abstractly or metaphorically, and their ability to think logically is often seriously impaired. As the following example illustrates, in such impaired thinking, opposites can coexist.

> I was extremely unhappy. I felt myself getting younger; the system wanted to reduce me to nothing. Even as I diminished in body and age, I discovered that I was nine centuries old. For to be nine centuries old actually meant being not yet born. That is why the nine centuries did not make me feel at all old; quite the contrary. (Torrey, 1983, p. 20)

Delusions and hallucinations are probably the best-known symptoms of schizophrenia. They also occur at times in the acute stages of affective disorder. Delusions and hallucinations are the patients' best attempts to give meaning to the confusion in their heads. Torrey (1983) defines delusions as "false ideas believed by the patient and not by other people in his/her culture and which cannot be corrected by reason" (p. 24). The overacuteness of the senses and the impaired ability to logically synthesize incoming thoughts and stimuli seem to lie behind the delusions. As we noted earlier, Anscombe (1987) sees delusions as the result of a person's inability to maintain control over her or his attentional directions, resulting in a sense of being captured by things in the environment. Because these things have such salience for these patients, they endow them with a heightened sense of significance. The following examples reveal such a tendency:

> It dawned on David that the CIA was listening to most of his thoughts wherever he went, even sometimes during sleep. David could not think privately in words. His thoughts in words gave rise to subvocal movements that produced specific patterns of sounds during breathing; the patterns were immediately picked up and deciphered by hidden CIA electronic equipment. (Zelt, 1981, p. 529)

> The walk of a stranger on the street would be a "sign" to me which I must interpret. Every face in the windows of a passing streetcar would be engraved on my mind, all of them concentrating on me and trying to pass me some sort of a message. (MacDonald, 1960)

> I was suddenly confronted with an overwhelming conviction that I had discovered the secrets of the universe, which were rapidly being made plain with incredible lucidity. The truths discovered seemed to be known immediately and directly, with

absolute certainty. I had no sense of doubt or awareness of the
possibility of doubt. (Anonymous, 1955, p. 679)

Freedman (1974) found a variety of miscellaneous disturbances in memory, language, and speech in the 50 autobiographical reports that he studied. He found that rather than immediately
comprehending words spoken to them, patients experienced a lag
between hearing the word, recalling its meaning, and formulating
an answer. Speech required great concentration and conscious
effort.

> Sometimes when people speak to me, my head is overloaded. It's
> too much to hold at once. It goes out as quick as it goes in. It
> makes you forget what you just heard because you can't get
> hearing it long enough. It's just words in the air unless you can
> figure it out from their faces. (Freedman, 1974, p. 338)

Freedman reported that the sense of time of some of his
subjects was also distorted during the acute stages of their disorders. Some said that they had lost all sense of time, and with it, all
notions about logic, order, and sequence.

> . . . my time sense was disturbed. This was the result of intense
> cerebral activity in which inner experiences took place at greatly
> increased speed, so that much more than usual happened per
> minute of external time. The result was to give an effect of slow
> motion . . . The speeding up of my inner experiences provided in
> this way an apparent slowing down of the external world. (Freed-
> man, 1974, p. 338)

Changes in Emotions

According to Torrey (1983), exaggerated feelings usually are not
found in schizophrenic patients beyond the early stages. If they do
persist, it is more likely that the person has a mood disorder. Guilt
may be found in the early stages of schizophrenia and is very
common in depression.

> Moral tensions returned in full force. I am haunted by a sense of
> guilt; my conscience gives me no rest, even when there do not
> seem to be any particularly grievous sins upon it. Whatever I am
> doing I feel I ought to be doing something else. I worry perpetu-
> ally about my past sins and failure; not for a moment can I forget
> the mess I seem to have made of my life. However I may pray for

forgiveness, no forgiveness comes. Eventually the terrors of Hell approach. (Landis & Mettler, 1952, p. 5)

Fear is frequently described by patients as often pervasive and nameless, and without any object (Torrey, 1983).

My fear was based fundamentally upon a terror of myself, of what was happening to me, of the helplessness that was over-powering my faculties . . . I began to be afraid of people, of my family and of my friends; not because of what they represented, I soon learned, but because of my own inability to cope with ordinary human contacts. (Landis & Mettler, 1955, p. 251)

Fears usually accompany depression and schizophrenia and may be one of the most disabling components of these disorders. There may be feelings of impending death, disease, or disaster. Fear may also be blended with other emotional states such as unreality, anger, or reverence. Fears can be all-pervasive and all-powerful, blotting out all other feelings and interests. When in the throes of fear, the whole person is immobilized, while seeking a "center of safety" (Landis & Mettler, 1955).

The most characteristic changes in schizophrenia are inappro-priate emotions or flattening emotions. One of the most tragic consequences of this disease is the impaired ability to empathize with other people (Torrey, 1983).

During class, in the quiet of the work period, I heard the street noises—a trolley passing, people talking, a horse neighing, a horn sounding, each detached, immovable, separated from its source, without meaning. Around me the other children, heads bent over their work, were robots or puppets, moved by an invisible mech-anism. On the platform, the teacher, too, talking, gesticulating, rising to write on the blackboard, was a grotesque jack-in-the-box. (Anscombe, 1987, p. 254)

Alterations in sense of self are fairly common in schizophrenia. McGrath (1984) describes this strange feeling: "If I want to reach out to touch me, I feel nothing but a slippery coldness, yet I sense that it is me. . . . my existence seems undefined—more a mirage that I keep reaching for, but never can touch" (p. 638). Other patients report having difficulty separating the real from the unreal:

It was just that sometimes I had a terrific sense of unreality. Suddenly I found myself in the present and all the immediate cords to the present had been severed. Like when someone wakes up in a strange room. Except that I had lived in the room for months. I often felt dazed. (Landis & Mettler, 1955, p. 361)

What is it like to be depressed? George Fish, a mental health advocate and freelance writer, offered to share his experience. In a personal communication to the author (June 7, 1987), Fish said that he wanted to cause the reader "to enter to the best of his/her ability into the world of the chronically depressed, to make the reader . . . *live*, even if ever so briefly, the life of someone suffering from chronic depression." Elsewhere, he writes:

> Being chronically depressed is like being trapped inside a bare, white room, a seamless monotony from which there is no escape. In fact, it is this which is the essence of depression; the despair of absolute *nothingness*, of being trapped in a complete void. Nothingness: that is depression—no color, no light, no spirit, no substance, no reality, no fantasy, just the paralyzing sense of despair that nothing, *absolutely nothing*, can be done to change it. (Fish, 1985, p. 2)

Another sufferer writes:

> I reached a stage where almost my entire world consisted of tortured contemplation of things which brought pain and unutterable depression. My brain after a short time, became sore with real physical soreness, as if it had been rubbed with sandpaper until it was raw. It felt like a bleeding sponge. (MacDonald, 1960, p. 218)

About a third of the persons who have depression go on to have mania as well. A person experiencing mania feels imbued with energy, optimism, and self-confidence. Mood is euphoric, expansive, and often infectious, as Papolos and Papolos (1987) note and illustrate with the following examples:

> One night I woke up and started feeling good again. I felt I could do more with my time, that anything was possible. I felt alive and vital, full of energy. My senses seemed alive, colors were very bright, they hit me harder. Things appeared clearcut, I noticed things I had never noticed before. There was a feeling of exhilaration, a sense of union with the whole world. (p. 18)

In time, the acute phases of mental illness come under control and some of the more severe kinds of suffering abate. But as more energy is available to attend to the external world again and to put life back together, a range of new problems present themselves: how to integrate the acute phases of illness into experiences of a life span, how to deal with chronicity and stigma, and how to cope with the loss of hopes and dreams of a once healthy self. Families as a most important support system can help their ill relative make the necessary new adjustments.

Coming to Terms with Life

The intrusion of a severe mental illness in a person's life presents a formidable adaptive challenge. As we come to understand it better, we marvel that people with mental illnesses do as well as they do. For a few there may be a temptation to retreat to the delusional system that once gave meaning and importance to their lives:

> I really missed my illness when I was free of it. I guess what I missed most was the sense of mystery. My visual hallucinations filled me with a sense of wonder and awe, as well as scaring me more than any horror could have done.

> My illness was a great ego builder. Just think, God thought I was so special that he was punishing me like this. It was quite a letdown to find that my "religious experiences" were all a fraud and that people weren't really writing songs and magazine articles about me. (MacKinnon, 1977, p. 427)

Facing the new realities of life in the community presents a myriad of new problems to overcome.

Developing an Acceptable Identity

Harris and Bergman (1984) work aggressively with highly disabled clients newly released from institutions into the community. They find that getting better is a mixed blessing for many of their clients. They become frightened about the future, but realize they cannot return to institutional settings. They quote one client who said, "I cannot go back there. I am not like those people anymore" (p. 31). Removing or changing patients' identities may temporarily leave them without a sense of who they are. The resultant confusion can make them feel worse than the patient role they are seeking to abandon.

> If you meet somebody and they say what do you do all day and you say I go to therapy, they look at you like you're nuts, and sometimes it's hard to tell people that you go to therapy instead of work. They look at you funny. (Godschalx, 1986, p. 75)

As people manage a degree of recovery, they begin to see the profound loss of opportunity, achievement, and material success that they have suffered. Upon return to the community, they meet old acquaintances and friends and compare themselves to their successful brothers and sisters. They may see themselves as chronic losers in life. Patients in Godschalx's (1986) study talk about their losses:

> I want to get a nice car and a house and a wife ... that's impossible though. I don't think any chick will ever love me. Real true like everybody else. I thinks it's impossible. I didn't think it was impossible before. (p. 68)

> It's scary when I think I can't have a child and my parents are gone. I don't know who I would live with and I don't know who I could love next, well ... I just think of committing suicide to be truthful with you. But I figure if I had a little girl it would pull me through. I would have somebody to love and care for. I'm sure she would love me. (p. 68)

Recovering patients must be allowed to grieve for their lost hopes and dreams. They need a great deal of support from families and professionals to see them through this painful period lest they yield to hopelessness and despair, or possible suicide.

The fortunate ones are those who are able to return to a former identity that had meaning for them—a vocation, a family role, or an artistic skill by which they identified themselves. For many, these are no longer viable options. Increasingly, former patients find themselves doing meaningful work in helping others who are mentally ill. For example, Cathy King (1987) found a positive identity for herself as director of a patient self-help organization, the Marin Network of Mental Health Clients. Esso Leete (1987), after surviving "fifteen hospitalizations, twice as many doctors, twenty different medications, and almost every kind of therapy imaginable" (p. 84), now is a full-time employee at Fort Logan, a state hospital in Denver, to which she was once involuntarily committed. In addition, she started the Denver Social Support Group, in which members help each other cope with mental illness. "The realization that *it can be done* is one of the most important aspects of our work," Leete says, "for success will never be realized if it cannot be imagined" (p. 88).

Learning Management of Illness and Self-Care

A part of successful adaptation to mental illness involves the recognition of symptomatology and the making of appropriate responses to handle it, as the following example illustrates:

> I have gotten so I can recognize when trouble is going to hit. Every single thing "means" something. This kind of symbolic thinking is exhausting. Fears begin to build up . . . panic, when alone, is at odds with the fear of people. I have a sense that everything is more vivid and important. (Brundage, 1983, p. 5841)

Leete (1987) has learned to accept her mental illness and has developed skills to help her cope:

> Stress plays a major role in my illness. Whatever I can do to decrease or avoid high-stress situations or environments is helpful in controlling my symptoms. Too much free time, leisure time, I have found to be detrimental; regular structured activity, however, is immeasurably important for my functioning and overall outlook in life, especially when combined with ongoing encouragement and support. When one has a chaotic inner existence, a predictable daily schedule is helpful. (p. 89)

> In addition, it is important to recognize my own personal warning signs of relapse, those symptoms that may signal a return to a more active and problematic stage of my illness. In any case, they include decreased sleep, trouble with concentration, forgetfulness, increased paranoia, more frequent voices, irritability, and being more easily overwhelmed by my environment. (p. 89)

Warning signals may vary from patient to patient but learning to recognize them is a big hurdle in living with mental illness.

Godschalx (1986) identified sources of insecurity in patients and strategies that they can use to overcome them. She found patients to be anxious about the terror of hallucinations, about the sense of being different, about possible loss of control, and about the likelihood of being victimized. Patients tried to deal with these insecurities by monitoring their own internal tensions, structuring their own thinking, and getting emotional support. They tried to focus on positive thinking, self-talk, using activity to structure thought, and taking psychotropic medication. Leete (1987) describes the use of family to assist in monitoring symptoms:

> It has been invaluable to me to have someone with whom I can "test reality," usually my husband. I let him know my perceptions and he gives me feedback; he serves as my sounding board and is my link with reality. I am then able to consider the possibility that my perceptions may not be accurate, and I modify my response accordingly if I wish. (p. 88)

Coping with Stigma

As if coping with a severe disabling illness were not enough, people with mental illnesses are endlessly plagued by social rejection because of their illness. Stigma is an ugly reality, Flynn (1987) pointed out in a recent article, for it means that those struggling to overcome these disorders face a constant series of rejections and exclusions. The destructive effects are many: People cannot find housing, they are discriminated against in employment, they are unable to get health insurance, and many mental health professionals choose not to work with them. Brundage (1983), a 44-year-old nurse and former patient, states:

> The stigma of mental illness was the harder thing to overcome for me. I am embarrassed to admit how prejudiced I was. My attitude was, "It's O.K. for others, but it could not happen to me." (p. 584)

Leete (1987) also stresses the severe burden patients suffer because of stigma:

> An ever-present obstacle keeping someone who has been psychiatrically labeled from reaching his or her potential is stigma. There is nothing more devastating, discrediting and disabling to a person recovering from mental illness than stigma. In addition to the handicaps posed by our illness, we must constantly deal with the barriers erected by society. (p. 88)

Godschalx (1986) found that participants used many coping strategies to manage their perceptions of being mentally ill. Some chose to ignore the problem and attend to other aspects of their lives:

> I think I have an appointment the next day and I go in. Then I drive off and never think about it again. I don't got anything to hold onto. (*Pause*) I go see ladies and I remember them. I think about them all the time. (p. 55)

Others in Godschalx's sample chose to work on their problems and to expect things to be different in the future: "I think of myself as a normal person with some problems. I've come a long way to where I feel I'm not as bad as I used to be" (p. 55).

For most of her subjects, Godschalx found, having a "mental illness" was not acceptable. She noted patients constantly making efforts to find ways in which they were like everyone else.

King (1987), in her "Dissolving the Barriers: Reflections on Coming out of the Closet," illustrates a number of ways in which patients attempt to transcend the stigma of mental illness and the indignities it imposes. For example, they demonstrate their ability to control their own lives:

> They said it couldn't be done—that we mental patients would never be capable of organizing to share in determining the course of our lives ("They are too disorganized, passive, dependent, inept, can't relate to others, etc., etc., etc."), but gradually, testing the waters, feeling our way, putting on our identity piece by piece, with the encouragement of others sympathetic, we're starting to make it happen. . . . "Good heavens! The inmates are running the asylum." (p. 7)

King talks of discovering the importance of encountering a fellowship of others of "her own kind." She experienced a phenomenon hitherto rare in her life, a sense of really belonging to a group. She was able to say, with its support, "Hey! I've had an interesting life! I'm special! I have something to offer! I am worth the space I take up on this earth" (p. 7). As one way of transcending the negative image of mental illness, King took pleasure in "shocking the straights" and testing the limits of what might be tolerated:

> Understandably enough, I became somewhat cocky at this point, and began to manifest one of the primary symptoms of emer-

gence from the closet: A certain amount of exhibitionism based on a strange new pride in the stigmatizing features which had resulted in my real and imagined oppression.

Admittedly possessing an appetite for precariousness, in the style of acrobatics upon a precipice, I took pleasure in myself in situations where it would likely be unavoidable that I would exhibit some behavior or language that would "give me away" and would then secretly revel in observing people's reactions— the dumbfounded looks, the embarrassed attempts to cover for me, the abruptly terminated conversations, the changing of sub- jects. I was simultaneously having a joke on people, turning the tables by being the one relatively in control of myself while they were losing it. (pp. 7–8)

Summary

This synthesis of first-person accounts of the phenomenological side of mental illness is intended to help mental health profession- als understand the schizophrenic or depressive experience, so that they in turn can help families augment their empathic relationships with their disabled member. Knowing what people with these men- tal illnesses go through has an additional positive effect. It com- mands our respect for the strength, courage, and persistence of mentally ill people who struggle so long to overcome their difficul- ties and make a life for themselves.

CHAPTER 7

Treatments for Mental Illness

There is a marked trend in modern psychiatry to work closely with families of the mentally ill in planning and monitoring treatment of the ill member. It is now recognized that families are likely to be the best authorities on what their relative is like, since they are often in a position to observe their relative in a range of situations over the course of time. In order for families to play an effective collaborative role with providers, they want and need to be fully educated about the nature and purposes of treatments to be used and their potential values and limitations.

Medications

During the decade of the 1950s, the introduction of several new drugs revolutionized psychiatry. Psychiatrists discovered that they were able to treat a variety of serious mental illnesses that had hitherto been untreatable, with the result that the afflicted and their families have been spared considerable anguish and society has been saved billions of dollars in institutional care. During the first half of this century the number of patients in mental hospitals steadily increased nationally from 150,000 to about 500,000. In 1956, the first year that these drugs were widely used in this country, the upward trend began reversing itself, and at present the hospital census hovers around 175,000 (Lickey & Gordon, 1983).

In spite of this impressive record, there have been resistances to drug treatments that are important to understand. One source of resistance has been the strong tradition of psychoanalysis and related psychodynamic theories, which favor talk therapies as treatment for mental illnesses. Following the leadership of Freud and his followers, it has been widely assumed that mental illnesses arise from disturbed psychological processes acquired in child-hood that result from problematic family relationships. Another common objection is that medications do not cure, which they do not, but it has been assumed erroneously that talk therapies do. Other common complaints are that these drugs turn patients into "zombies" and/or are only used to control patients (Lickey & Gordon, 1983). While no one is completely satisfied with the quality of drugs now available, research has clearly demonstrated that these medications do control symptoms and do make it possible for most patients to return to family and community.

Medications for Schizophrenia

Most psychiatrists believe that neuroleptics or antipsychotic medi-cations are the treatment of choice for people with schizophrenia. The antipsychotic properties of chlorpromazine were discovered by accident in France in the 1950s, and the drug was first marketed in the United States under the trade name Thorazine in 1954. The development of other antipsychotic drugs followed rapidly. Some, like chlorpromazine, are members of the phenothiazine family. Others, such as haloperidol (trade name, Haldol), are chemically unrelated to chlorpromazine (Lickey & Gordon, 1983; Andreasen, 1984). Some of the most common trade names are Thorazine, Prolixin, Mellaril, Stelazine, and Navane.

BENEFICIAL EFFECTS OF MEDICATION

For most patients the neuroleptic drugs work well to reduce or eliminate hallucinations and delusional thinking. Patients become more emotionally responsive, pay more attention and respond more to others, and improve their hygiene and self-care. For some people the improvement is quite dramatic, for others changes come more slowly, and for a few (about 10%) there is little or no response. Drugs differ to some extent in the amount of sedation and the kinds of side effects produced. While no one drug is considered the best for all patients, individual patients may re-spond better to one or more drugs than to others.

Neuroleptics work best to control the so-called "positive symp-toms," that is, the confused thinking, strange behavior, irritability, and disorganization. Neuroleptics are believed to have little effect on the "negative symptoms," such as low motivation, impoverished speech, and flattened affect. These troublesome symptoms are a cause for a great deal of concern, and research in this area is increasing.

Side effects are a potential with all medications and antipsychotic medications are no exception. While most side effects are uncomfortable but not serious, there is also the possibility of serious side effects. Torrey (1983) conveniently classified side effects into five types:

1. *Common and less serious.* These are discomforts of which patients often complain when first taking neuroleptics—dry mouth, constipation, blurring of vision, and drowsiness. These side effects usually go away after the first few weeks. More troublesome are such disturbances as restlessness (called akathisia), stiffness and diminished spontaneity (called akinesia), slurring of speech, and hand and feet tremors.

Some patients suffer from dystonia, which is the involuntary muscular contractions that produce strange movements of face, neck, tongue, and back. A particularly distressing manifestation of dystonia involves the eyes, which may roll uncontrollably or become fixed, looking toward the ceiling. This condition tends to respond quickly to anticholinergic drugs such as benztropine mesylate (trade name, Cogentin) and trihexyphenidyl hydrochloride (trade name, Artane). Restlessness, stiffness, and tremors also respond in varying degrees to these drugs. When patients do not respond, it may be necessary to try an alternative antipsychotic medication.

2. *Uncommon and less serious.* Side effects in this category include menstrual changes in women or discharge from the breasts. Both are caused by changes in the pituitary glands, and, while annoying, are not serious enough to warrant stopping the drugs. Changes in sexual functioning can occur as a side effect of neuroleptics, but how often they occur and how serious a problem they seem to be is a matter of dispute. It is difficult to determine when these problems are a consequence of antipsychotic drugs and when they may be due to schizophrenia.

3. *Common and more serious.* There are three side effects that are fairly common and potentially serious. One is oversensitivity to the sun, in that the person may burn easily. This requires sunscreens and other kinds of protection from direct exposure to sunlight. Another potentially serious side effect is fainting when the person goes from a lying to a sitting position. Weight gain is a third

common and more serious side effect of medication. In some cases the gain may be so serious that it becomes necessary to discontinue medication.

4. *Uncommon and serious.* Antipsychotic medications, Torrey warns, may have serious and, rarely, fatal side effects. Fortunately, these are uncommon. Damage to blood-forming organs, which decreases the number of white blood cells, can result in susceptibility to infections. Blockage of urinary tracts and intestinal obstruction have been reported. Convulsions have also been reported and, rarely, abnormalities in heart functioning.

5. *Tardive dyskinesia.* This syndrome has received much attention in recent years. The condition usually develops in older people with schizophrenia and those who have been on neuroleptic drugs for a long time. It consists of involuntary movements of the tongue and mouth, such as chewing movements, pushing the cheek out with the tongue, and smacking the lips. Occasionally there are jerky, purposeless movements of the arms or legs and sometimes the whole body. The frequency and seriousness of tardive dyskinesia is a hotly debated topic. Estimates of frequency are compounded by the fact that the symptoms of tardive dyskinesia can be caused by the schizophrenia as well as the drugs used to treat it. The most informed estimate to date, Torrey says, is that 13% of chronic schizophrenic patients suffer from some degree of drug-induced tardive dyskinesia. In the great majority of cases the early symptoms of tardive dyskinesia will disappear when antipsychotic medication is stopped. Hence, families and patients will have to weigh the potential risks of tardive dyskinesia against the risks of recurrent schizophrenia.

MEDICATION MANAGEMENT

Neuroleptic medications do not cure schizophrenia. Once the acute symptoms are brought under control, patients are usually required to remain on maintenance doses of medication for an indefinite future. There is always a temptation to cease medication once symptoms diminish, in which case relapse and rehospitalization will then be likely. Families and patients must be advised of the risks of discontinuation of drugs.

Modern psychiatry involves the family (or surrogate family) in monitoring medication and its effects between physician visits. Upon assuming this responsibility, families quite naturally have a lot of questions, such as those about addiction. They should be told that drug addiction is not one of the side effects of neuroleptics, and that patients do not develop tolerance for the drug nor do they suffer severe withdrawal symptoms when it is discontinued.

Families also want to know which drug is best and what the correct dosage should be. As mentioned previously, there is no evidence that one antipsychotic drug is more effective than another. Although these drugs vary in potency, less potent drugs can be as effective as more potent ones, especially when used in higher dosages. The physician usually selects the neuroleptic because of its particular side effects, as well as its particular therapeutic effects (Lickey & Gordon, 1983). Families should be good observers of their relative and report from week to week such things as clarity of thinking, alertness, and activity as evidence of the effectiveness of the drugs prescribed. They should also be alert to side effects and report them to the doctor. Sometimes change to a different neuroleptic is indicated, but this can be determined only after a trial period of several weeks.

One of the most frustrating and baffling problems in medication management is medication noncompliance. This we will examine in some detail in a later chapter.

Medications for Mood Disorders

The effectiveness of drugs for the treatment of mood disorders has now been firmly established through research. Mood swings are prevented or become less frequent; life often returns to a high degree of normalcy. In 1949 lithium was discovered, and shortly after the antidepressant drugs became available.

LITHIUM THERAPY

Lithium is the drug of choice for treating mania. The medication literally makes the difference between a life of chaos and disruption and a life of stability and productivity (Papolos & Papolos, 1987). Lithium calms manic patients. Continued lithium therapy protects them against future manic episodes and future depressive episodes as well. While there is no cure for bipolar illness at this time, lithium is a very effective way to control it. This means that if people stop taking their lithium, manic or depressive symptoms are likely to recur.

Lithium does not work for everyone who needs it. It is estimated that 80% of all manic patients respond to lithium. Psychiatrists do not know how to account for the failures. Improper diagnosis is always a possibility, but there is no direct evidence to support that contention. Another explanation is that there are biologically different types of manic depression—one category includes those who are responsive to lithium and another, those who are nonresponsive (Lickey & Gordon, 1983).

Certain laboratory tests are necessary before starting lithium to insure its safe use and to determine how one's system functions. Evaluation of kidney and thyroid functions is essential. A doctor familiar with lithium therapy is best able to determine the correct medication for each patient. In order for lithium to be effective, the proper concentration in the blood must be held. Too little can be ineffective, but too much can be toxic. Therefore, the person taking lithium must have blood tests in order to determine the exact lithium concentration for her or his blood. The physician will provide some precise directions for preparing for these tests. At first, blood tests may be needed as often as once a week, but once the serum levels have been stabilized, a blood level may be needed only once a month or less often (Papolos & Papolos, 1987).

Lithium is nonsedating and nonaddictive. It is safe at appropriate levels, which can be insured by maintaining a normal sodium balance. Diuretics that cause the kidneys to excrete sodium, and low salt diets must be avoided. Most of the common side effects are harmless and relatively easy to manage. Gastrointestinal symptoms such as nausea, vomiting, and diarrhea may occur but tend to subside in a few days. These side effects can usually be alleviated through adjustment of dosage or timing of administration. Taking the tablets on a full stomach or taking them with a glass of milk may also be effective. There may also be fine tremors of the hands, thirst, and frequent elimination. Sometimes there is a tendency for weight gain that requires constant monitoring of caloric intake (Papolos & Papolos, 1987).

ANTIPSYCHOTIC MEDICATIONS

Patients who suffer from mania or psychotic depression may also suffer from delusions and hallucinations. Neuroleptic drugs, such as are used for schizophrenia, are then used. While lithium might prevent such states from occurring in the future, lithium takes from 10 to 14 days to become effective. Antipsychotic drugs work much faster and insure comfort and safety in the initial stages. Once the lithium level is built up, the neuroleptic medication can be gradually discontinued.

ANTIDEPRESSANTS

A physician can treat a patient suffering from depression in one of several ways. He can use tricyclic antidepressants, monoamine oxidase inhibitors (MAOIs), or electroconvulsive therapy. Tricyclic antidepressants are the most commonly used and the best researched. Elavil, Sinequan, Tofranil, and Vivactil are trade names of commonly prescribed drugs. Papolos and Papolos (1987) note that patients have individual responses to tricyclic antidepressants but that a fairly common sequence is: improvement in sleep, changes noted by other people, and, in a couple of weeks, patient awareness that symptoms have alleviated. The most common side effects are dry mouth, drowsiness, constipation, and light-headedness when rising quickly from a lying or sitting position.

MAOIs are somewhat controversial in this country. They tend to be used when other drugs fail to achieve adequate responses. There are a number of dietary prohibitions that must be observed to ward off the possibility of dangerously high blood pressure. Some of the prohibited foods are: cheese, yogurt, liver, corned beef, and salted fish. In addition, a person taking an MAOI should take no other medications unless cleared by a physician (Papolos & Papolos, 1987).

Modern electroconvulsive therapy (ECT) is a safe and effective treatment for depression. It relieves depression rapidly, and it may be lifesaving. It has a higher success rate for severe depression than any other form of treatment. The patient is put to sleep and given a muscle relaxant. A small current of electricity is passed through the brain producing a mild seizure. Upon awakening the patient may experience a brief period of confusion and some memory loss, which will clear up within a month. Papolos and Papolos (1987) feel that ECT does not deserve its negative reputation. Most people who have had ECT say they would agree to having ECT again.

Medications for Severe Anxiety

The antianxiety drugs are some of the most widely prescribed in medicine. Trade names of commonly used drugs are Valium, Librium, Ativan, and Xanax. These drugs calm people without sedating them or making them feel high. They have only minimal side effects and minimal long-term risks. The only serious long-term side effect is psychological dependence, and perhaps physiological dependence when taken in very high doses. When the drugs are stopped abruptly, patients sometimes show withdrawal symptoms such as tremulousness, agitation, or seizures (Andreasen, 1984).

Medications for Borderline Personality Disorder

There is much controversy about the treatment of borderline patients. There has been a strong emphasis on psychodynamic therapy in the past but there is now a readiness to begin thinking about some somatic therapies. At this time, there are advocates for the use of tricyclic antidepressants; MAOIs; and low doses of phenothiazine, lithium, and tegretol, but there has been very limited research in this area. Gunderson (1984) recommends that borderline patients with specific affective symptoms should receive antidepressants and those with apparent psychosis should receive neuroleptics. Gunderson reminds us that the origins and treatment of borderline personality is multidetermined and incompletely understood, and that there likely is a role for both psychological and biological causes and treatments.

Psychotherapy

The use of drugs in the treatment of mental illnesses has grown rapidly since 1949 when John F. C. Cabe reported some of his experiments with lithium. While some professionals believe that the only effective treatments are medications, most professionals in mental illness feel that certain kinds of psychotherapy can be beneficial, and when there is significant impairment that social rehabilitation can play an important role in treatment.

Psychotherapy for Schizophrenia

While there are those who strongly adhere to the idea that psychotherapy is useful in treating schizophrenia, there is no evidence to support that contention. Research is difficult in this area because the various techniques of psychotherapy are as numerous as the psychotherapists that perform them. Often evaluating the psychotherapies are the psychotherapists who are doing therapy. Rigorous studies are scarce but one well-designed study that is often quoted was conducted by May (1968) at Camarillo State Hospital in California. He found that adding psychotherapy to drug treatment accomplished nothing.

Torrey (1983) points out that insight therapy may not only be useless but it may also be detrimental. People with schizophrenia, already overwhelmed by internal and external stimuli, if asked to probe their unconscious motivations, could easily be overwhelmed by a flood of repressed material into consciousness.

Supportive counseling could be very helpful, once the most aggravated symptoms abate, to help patients pick up the threads of their lives again. Patients may need to learn or relearn how to make friends, where to find a place to live, what to tell friends about their illnesses, and how to get jobs (Lickey & Gordon, 1983). Supportive therapy consists primarily of friendship, advice, and practical help in securing services. Therapists can help patients accept the limitations of their illnesses and learn to successfully live in the community and lead as normal a life as possible. Group psychotherapy, like individual therapy, when focused on insight may precipitate a psychosis. Groups with a predominantly educational or social focus, however, may alleviate loneliness and help people cope with real life problems.

Psychotherapy for Mood Disorders

Papolos and Papolos (1987) believe that psychotherapy is a critical factor in the treatment of mood disorders. People with recurrent mood disorder suffer a very real loss of function and a loss of confidence and security. They each have an emotional response to their illness to which therapy can help them come to terms. Some patients have difficulty accepting the need for long-term medication. Most need help learning to recognize symptoms of an impending mood swing so that they can get help before relapse occurs. In an ongoing dialogue with a trusted professional, patients can regain their confidence in social situations and work through their painful humiliation over what they may have done during a manic episode (Papolos & Papolos, 1987).

Psychotherapy for Severe Anxiety

For the treatment of excessive anxiety, drugs should never be the only form of therapy. Because of the addiction risk associated with anti-anxiety drugs and the possible complication of alcohol, there is danger to a drugs-only approach (Lickey & Gordon, 1983). Patients should receive warm human support and strategies for coping with life stresses.

Psychotherapy for Borderline Personality Disorder

There is considerable controversy about the treatment of borderline personality. Gunderson (1984) says that it should be multimodal and should include psychotherapy and hospitalization plus medication. Interventions to help families are often warranted and sometimes group therapy can be useful.

Summary

Collaborative approaches to managing mental illness, in which families, patients, and providers work together in partnership are strongly recommended. But to be true partners means that all must be fully informed about mental illness and the treatments now available. They must know what the risks and benefits of various medications are and how to monitor them properly. They need to know the value of various individual and family therapies and criteria by which to choose therapists.

CHAPTER 8

Creating Supportive Environments

People with mental illnesses live almost continuously under overwhelming levels of stress, almost all of internal origin. Their lives are characterized by fearfulness and mistrust. They feel themselves at the mercy of forces beyond their control and often beyond their understanding. Hence, the most effective help that others can give is to create external environments that might have a salutary effect on a patient's inner turmoil.

It is instructive to relate what we have learned from patients about their experiences with stress to what leading stress theorists say about the conditions most likely to predispose people, in general, to becoming overstressed. High levels of stress are likely to occur, these theorists note, when: (1) there is an orientation to life in which internal and external events are not experienced as being predictable; (2) there is a demand–capability imbalance; and (3) there is great social ambiguity. Patients with mental illnesses are predisposed to all of these conditions of stress. The challenge is to find ways of creating environmental supports that can maximize the level of comfort of these patients and their capacities for performing at their highest levels.

Increasing a Sense of Coherence

Antonovsky's (1979) thesis that a central factor in creating a state of well being in human beings is their having a sense of coherence and predictability about life is useful in helping us understand patients with mental illnesses and their needs. Antonovsky says, "The sense of coherence is a global orientation that expresses the extent to which one has a pervasive, enduring though dynamic, feeling of confidence that one's internal and external environments are predictable and that there is a high probability that things will work out as well as can be expected" (p. 123). Accounts of patients' experiences with their illnesses teach us that many patients go through long periods of time when their "global orientations" are anything but coherent and predictable. Many see their world as capricious and incoherent.

Psychotic individuals suffer severe distortions of shape, size, color, space, and time. What is more, each of these may change without warning. We know that time and space form the foundations of social organization and all people have a need to be organized; however, the ability for organization is often unattainable for those with psychotic conditions (Burton, 1974). While appropriate medications can reduce perceptual distortions and cognitive confusion, a predictable and stable environment can supplement medication and further support the individual in achieving internal order. Families and other caregivers can help by giving attention to continuity of experience, predictability of events, and structure. Providers can teach families how to provide these conditions in their homes.

Continuity of Experience

People with mental illnesses often appear rigid and inflexible; they change direction with difficulty, since inordinate amounts of stress accompany change. We interpret this behavior as a response to internal chaos and an effort to compensate by resisting change. It is difficult to alter a life course with confidence when the ground beneath is constantly shifting; each change in life makes the ground shift further.

There must be planning for these people so that there is as much continuity in their lives as possible. Ideally, they should retain their treating psychiatrists over a long period of time, and they should be able to retain the same housing and other supports until they are truly ready for such changes. Our fragmented mental health systems deny these people the continuity that they need to regain confidence in the world and function well in it. The concepts of transitional housing and transitional work flies in the face of what we know about the need for stability and continuity. Whenever continuity is broken, there must be considerable support available until stability is restored again.

Mendel (1974) sees people with schizophrenia as lacking in historicity. By this he means that events do not remain with these patients; each experience, he says, is experienced as being brand new. They do not build up a body of lived history to give them a sense of continuity in their lives. Without a sense of prior experience, they cannot meet new challenges with confidence; they have great difficulty in anticipating and planning for events; and they have difficulty in being goal-directed and in profiting from experience. In addition, the practical problems of living with others become enormous when one has these deficits.

The failure of historicity leaves patients with a poor sense of time because they have not experienced an orderly flow of events. There has not been a lot written about how to help people with this problem. Patients will need much more help than just nagging them about the importance of planning ahead and the value society places on being on time. They will need considerable guidance in experiencing the flow of time and determining how much lead time is needed to arrive someplace on time. They may need to stay close to clocks and calendars and learn how to anticipate events.

Caregivers may want to try to open the door of the patient to her or his past and try to link the present to the future in order to create a sense of life's continuity. Talking about early family and school events might bring the past into focus. Some patients seem to enjoy remembering about their childhood, however, some families report that their relative becomes agitated when childhood memories are provoked. This may be due to their incomplete memory and confusion or it may be due to the pain of recalling a happier and more promising period in life.

Predictability of Events

Patients need to feel that life is relatively predictable, that there is a degree of lawfulness about their environment, that events are not all arbitrary. Families can augment this sense of predictability by providing consistency of responses to their vulnerable relative. This requires thinking through responses before they are made and communicating in clear and direct language. To the extent possible, plans made for visits, outings, shopping, and the like should be carried out with an enhanced sense of predictability in mind. Promises, and also threats, should be made with care for they too must be carried out lest the world seem capricious and unpredictable.

When events are predictable, anxiety is reduced. When the ill person is about to face an activity or event that she or he has not encountered before, anxiety can be reduced if the caregiver helps anticipate what the experience will be like. Patients may be re-assured that events are predictable with a fair degree of accuracy; thus, they can prepare for them. This gives a sense of some degree of control over events.

Form and Structure

When thinking lacks order and structure and the inner world is in turmoil, it is helpful if the outer world has form and structure. Patients having distortions in temporality and spaciality need structure to provide a sense of time and space. Definite expecta-tions with few decisions and few adjustments can be reassuring. Most patients function best given a daily routine with established times for meals, bedtime, and daily tasks, together with a weekly schedule with particular activities assigned to certain days. This gives a pattern and a sense of order to life.

Patients with schizophrenia have difficulty separating the rele-vant from the irrelevant; therefore, it is important to reduce the complexities in the environment so that the most important facets of existence stand out. Family caregivers must decide what few things are the most essential to family functioning and make those things salient for the patient. Things of lesser importance should be downplayed or ignored so that the really significant can be grasped. Language that has clarity and structure also helps to provide form and pattern to existence. By being selective about what is said to their relative, families model what is relevant and what is not.

Bringing Demand and Capability into Balance

Patients with major mental illnesses suffer significant brain dys-function that tragically interferes with their ability to cope with the ordinary demands of life. Patients' accounts of what it is like to be confused, hazy, and bewildered, unable to filter out excess stimuli or to focus attention where it is needed, are convincing evidence that these illnesses present a massive assault on competence. McCubbin and Patterson (1983) remind us that a significant "demand–capability imbalance" produces high levels of stress. For an environment to be supportive, there must be reasonable con-gruence between expectations and capability.

Reducing Stimulation

To the extent that a patient's dysfunction or inability to meet ordinary environmental demands is due to cognitive overload, confusion, and inability to focus, stimulation in the environment needs to be reduced. Too many people, too many activities, and too much tension overtaxes the individual's capacity to sort out stimuli and respond properly. Patients may feel too confused to fulfill ordinary expectations, resulting in an increasing sense of incompetence and rising tension.

Clarity and simplification of language matters a great deal. A patient who has difficulty processing information is greatly helped if family members modify their language to simple, clear, unambiguous statements, so that she or he can comprehend and respond appropriately. Circumlocution and confused and inconsistent statements should be avoided, as should also sorting out ideas or thinking out loud. Patients may be unfairly considered uncooperative or forgetful when they really have not understood what was said. Simple ideas presented one at a time, followed by careful observation to note what the patient has grasped, can help to avoid this kind of misunderstanding.

Bernheim and Lehman (1985) wisely caution us not to place unrealistic expectations on families with regard to communication lest we create for them a sense of failure and an unwillingness to speak openly and freely. "As with problem solving skills," they point out, "our view is that families of the mentally ill are generally no better or worse at communicating than other families. They simply face a greater challenge" (p. 103). These families may sometimes have a real struggle to get through to their highly symptomatic relatives and have equal difficulty in understanding what they are saying. It may be awkward at first to make the necessary language adjustments. It requires becoming self-conscious about speech and taking time to plan what is going to be said. Instructors may help by modeling desirable communication patterns, but they must also help families adapt these models to their natural way of speaking.

Of equal concern to the amount of stimulation, is the degree of intensity. Torrey (1983) illustrates, through patient statements, the fact that many patients have overacute senses. Ordinary levels of noise may be painful to them. While patients are in a vulnerable stage of their illness, it is important that environments are quieter and calmer. Holidays, weddings, and other family celebrations present a real challenge for finding ways of protecting vulnerable relatives without putting a damper on normal family activities.

The meaning that an event has to the patient is a crucial variable in the stress that is generated. Meanings of events, however, are very personal, and it is difficult to understand why some events appear more stressful than others. Sometimes the meaning may relate to the patient's delusional world. At other times the meaning may lie in the patient's interpretation of what the situation is demanding and her or his perceived incompetence to meet the demands. One parent, for example, expected his son to warmly welcome a cousin that he had not seen for a long time because they were of similar ages and had played together as small children. Nothing was further from the truth. The son objected strenuously and refused to see the cousin. One can only speculate why that situation was so threatening: Perhaps it painfully reminded him of earlier and more promising times in his life; possibly there was a failure of historicity and he was confused about events of those early years; maybe he felt that he measured up poorly against his cousin's achievements; or perhaps he felt incompetent in the needed social skills to meet the situation.

Sometimes in their anxiety about the patient or in their well-intentioned efforts to help her or him, other family members become overly intrusive. Constant inquiries about the patient's well-being or hovering over her or him can increase anxiety and the need for protective withdrawal. Families are advised to limit face-to-face contact and to express emotion in moderation. They may need to be encouraged to develop interests outside the home in order to divert some of their energy away from the patient. Work, hobbies, or community activities give them needed respite from focus on their relative, which will make it easier for them to maintain a calm and low-keyed approach during the time they are around her or him.

Because tolerance to stress and which events seem stressful varies so much from person to person, family members cannot merely rely on their own measure of what constitutes a stressful situation. In addition, they must learn to pick up cues from their relative. Some patients react to stress by becoming preoccupied and withdrawn; some by becoming agitated and angry. Some people show stress in their facial expression or body posture; others have difficulty sleeping or they complain of fatigue. Families soon learn the particular signs their relative gives when she or he is being overstressed.

Finally, people highly vulnerable to stress can themselves learn to anticipate which events they are unable to tolerate and thus avoid them. They can learn to find socially approved ways to escape from situations that overwhelm them. Families can share their own ways of coping with stressful situations with their relatives so that they can adapt them to their use. The following are a few suggestions the family can offer:

- Know whatever you can about a new situation before you enter it.
- Be well prepared in whatever you are planning to do.
- Allow plenty of time to approach the situation.
- Identify people whom you can call on for advice.
- Retreat temporarily if necessary.

This discussion should not be concluded without giving some attention to the importance of avoiding understimulation. Too little stimulation from the outside world can result in a surge of stimulation from within and a return of voices and delusional thinking. Some patients report that they can actively control some of their psychotic symptoms by a moderate amount of activity.

Setting Appropriate Expectations

Considerable stress can result when a family's expectations exceed what the patient is capable of doing. Although hospitalization may be brief and the most florid symptoms may ameliorate, the person may be far from well. Recuperation from a major breakdown is necessarily a slow process. After the initial stabilization, a period of inactivity, lethargy, and excessive sleep is common. Since it is hard for others to know how much complexity the patient can manage, it is wise to start off with minimal demands for personal care, chores, errands, and the like, and gradually increase the level of expectation with time. The expectation that the individual will return to school or work must often be delayed for some time.

Sometimes it is the patient who has expectations that are too high. Rather than throw cold water on unrealistic aspirations, it is better to encourage postponing them for a while. Families can help identify short-term goals that will eventually feed into long-term aspirations. They can try to keep the patient from projects that are doomed to failure, for such failures can be a major setback to recovery.

Keeping expectations reasonable should not be interpreted as being permissive of any and all behavior. Families have a right to expect that the ill person treats others in the household with respect and that she or he has some responsibilities that are within her or his capabilities. If nothing is asked, the disturbed relative may come to believe that she or he is more disabled than is actually the case. Other family members may resent the patient's privileged position in the family. The patient needs to feel that she or he is making a valued contribution as a member of the family.

Enhancing Self-Esteem

Inevitably, a major mental illness is battering to a person's self-esteem. Self-esteem may first suffer from trying to understand and behave competently in a world that has become confused and disorganized. The indignities of hospitalization can further injure self-worth. Furthermore, recovering from such assaults on the sense of personal worth is nearly impossible in a world that continues to stigmatize anyone with a mental illness.

It is not surprising to find that people with mental illnesses are highly sensitive to criticism. Criticism is seen by them as an assault on self-esteem. The self-concept of many patients is very fragile and even minor criticisms may have a disorganizing effect on the person. The central concern of expressed emotion theory is the number of critical comments made by families about their schizophrenic relative. Leaders in this field (Anderson, Reiss, & Hogarty, 1986; Brown, Birley, & Wing, 1972; Falloon, Boyd, & McGill, 1984; Leff & Vaughn, 1985) say that they have empirical data to show that excessive critical comments can be damaging and that they may be factors in relapse. Families are likely to be less critical when they understand the nature of mental illness and how it impairs the functioning of those so afflicted.

We should not underestimate, however, the formidable challenge that families face in trying to accommodate a highly disturbed and disturbing relative in their midst. Providers often underestimate how difficult it is to apply their well-meant advice in the natural setting of the home where several members' needs must be considered.

Developing an Acceptable Identity

"The intrusion of a significant illness, especially of a chronic and disabling nature," Feldman (1980) wrote, "is a major life crisis posing a formidable challenge to what was a workable adaptation to life" (p. 14). Feldman believes that it is necessary for patients to surrender the sick role with its passive object state for another identity—one that allows maximum independence and freedom of choice. The chronically ill person must be helped to give up a role of being "sick" for that of being "different." People with mental illnesses have the awesome task of learning to accept the fact that life will be irrevocably different, and that because of that difference, a new meaning and a new way of life must be found. In Feldman's words, "To discover a new meaning in life in the face of the dissolution of the old meaning, to accept the difference imposed by the illness, and to still maintain one's dignity and worth is the essence of the transition from sick to different" (p. 17). Such a transition demands a reorganization and acceptance of the self so that there is a purpose in living that transcends the limitations of the illness. This is a formidable challenge.

Harris and Bergman (1984), drawing on their extensive experience working with newly deinstitutionalized patients in the community, warn that there may be emotional and intrapsychic consequences for those with long-term hospitalizations now trying to adjust to the community. For many patients, the patient role, with its dependence on others, has become a way of life; it has become their only identity. Patients may neither feel secure about living in the community nor do they feel that they can return to institutionalized living again. Their identities as patients have changed, but they do not feel secure in the new identities of coping adults. Removing or changing the patient identity, Harris and Bergman conclude, may temporarily if not permanently leave the individual without a sense of who she or he is and where she or he fits.

Harris and Bergman (1984) report that many of the patients react with overwhelming fear. Some prefer staying in the institution rather than facing the cold, cruel world. When patients shed patient roles, many experience profound feelings of loss. Some regret the loss of a delusional system that gave them a measure of comfort. Some grieve for the wasted years of their lives, knowing that they have missed out on education, good jobs, marriage, and homes. These patients need much help in overcoming a sense of hopelessness and despair. The answer, of course, does not lie in return to institutionalization, rather clinicians must prepare themselves for dealing with the crucial identity problems that will occur. They need to learn how to be helpful to families who have the painful task of helping their loved one adjust to the new realities.

Godschalx (1986) studied patients with schizophrenia from a phenomenological point of view and found many of them to be struggling with issues of identity. A number of them had great difficulty deciding what was wrong with them. Their responses varied from having "nervous breakdowns," having trouble with "spells" or "anxiety," or having "mental problems." Godschalx found no relationship between those who acknowledged a mental illness and either happiness or level of functioning.

Godschalx (1986) explored the various ways that patients tended to cope with the stressful fact that they had a mental illness. She found that the most common strategy was for them to express the ways in which they resembled everybody else. Some had chosen to ignore it and live; others had chosen to work on it; and still others had hoped for improvements in the future. Many saw themselves as nearly normal because "everybody has problems." All of these strategies tend to preserve self-esteem and lead to the development of hope. Patients reported finding meaning in life through a sense of accomplishment and by being useful.

In an earlier work, Godschalx (1985) examined the literature on the most desirable coping strategies for patients with schizophrenia and concluded that, perhaps, the healthiest way for clients to come to terms with the illness is to acknowledge the losses that they had suffered, deal with the grief that follows such a recognition, and work out a new adaptation to life. She notes that the patient may go through an extended period of sadness, tearfulness, lack of motivation, and possibly suicidal ideation before a new direction can be managed. Families should be in a position to support the patient in her or his long period of painful adjustment.

Some patients choose a pattern of avoidance as a way to cope with the unacceptable aspects of mental illness. A nondebilitating, defensive style seems to work best for them. They compartmentalize the part of life that has to do with mental illness, medication, and disability checks, and focus most of their time on daily activities and relationships. They show little or no curiosity about their illness and only during periods when psychotic symptoms increase significantly do these patients experience anxiety, helplessness, and decreased self-esteem. Once psychiatric symptoms are gone, they again successfully ignore the illness.

To rebuild one's sense of identity requires a reconsideration of values and a reassessment of what is important in life. Patients may find that some of the things that they value are still possible even with the limitations of their illness. Fortunate are those who can revive an earlier talent or skill such as in music, art, athletics, or nature study, for through the use of these talents, an identity is possible. In addition, people with mental illnesses need to be helped to see themselves as unique and interesting personalities in their own right, who have as only one attribute that of having a mental illness. For families and therapists, Godschalx (1985) points out, "Helping clients with chronic mental illnesses discover personal meaning in life that transcends the limitations of their illness is, indeed, the challenge of chronicity" (p. 406).

Summary

The purpose of this chapter was to explore with family educators ways of helping families to create supportive environments. The foundation material for this exploration was developed in Chapter 6, where we focused on the experiences that patients report about living with their disorders. We found that high levels of stress and anxiety are suffered due to the discontinuity in their lives, their lack of self-esteem due to inability to perform at expected levels, and the ambiguity in identity and social roles. And we noted that appropriately supportive environment can serve to offset or compensate for the patients' difficulties in functioning.

We concluded, in this chapter, that a supportive environment is characterized by:

- Continuity and predictability.
- Adequate structure and form.
- Limited amount and intensity of stimulation.
- Clear and calm communication.
- Appropriate expectations.
- Encouragement and positive regard.

CHAPTER 9

Coping with Crisis Situations

Living with mental illness means living on the edge of crises that could happen at any time. Families frequently say, "living with mental illness is like living at the edge of a volcano"; "we are always expecting that the other shoe will drop"; or "we live in dread that something terrible is about to happen." Unfortunately, when crises come, most families face them alone. The system is not yet prepared to be responsive. Hence, practitioners need to know about all of the resources available in their communities for crises situations and how they can be most quickly accessed.

In this chapter we discuss several kinds of critical problems that can lead to crises. To the extent that we can successfully intervene in these serious situations, crises may be aborted.

Medication Noncompliance

Even though most patients with mental illnesses respond well to psychotropic medications, a sizable percentage of them will fail to stay on their prescribed medication regimens. This becomes one of the most baffling and frustrating problems that families and professionals face, for almost invariably the patient will become psychotic, a crisis eventually will arise, and it will precipitate a need for hospitalization. Families repeatedly seek help from professionals regarding this dilemma. Diamond (1984) has prepared one of the most useful sets of guidelines for achieving medication compliance to appear in the literature. We draw liberally from his work.

We must start, he says, with the steps for increasing compliance that would apply to any patient population: Be sure the purpose is clear to the patient, that side effects are rapidly treated, that the patient can afford the medication, and that medication instructions are clear. Diamond offers additional guidelines he found to be useful:

1. Put the medication in the context of the patient's life. Most psychiatric patients want their lives to change in some way. If they can see medications as helping them to accomplish the changes that they want, they may be willing to put up with side effects and the inconvenience of taking medication. The proposed benefits of medication must fit into the patient's life in some concrete way. If the patient says that she or he wants to sleep better, feel less anxious at social functions, or concentrate better, make the patient aware that medications may help in doing these things.

2. Be concerned about compliance. Ask patients what medications they are taking and how much. It will be found frequently that they are taking either more or less than prescribed. It is important to know why they chose to make these adjustments in medication, for patients usually have a good reason for doing so. It is also a possibility that noncompliance is a matter of forgetting, in which case there is a need for a variety of practical suggestions such as: Take medication at the same time every day or along with some other regular predictable activity, simplify medication regimens as much as possible, and/or package medications in individual envelopes or containers. Finally, it may be necessary to ask someone else to dispense medication—the staff of a day program, a roommate, or a family member. The use of Prolixin Decanoate injections that need to be administered only once in every 4 weeks is a solution for some.

3. Make sure that the patient, the family, and other agencies of the mental health team are all informed about the medication. It is important for all to know what the medications can and cannot do. It may be necessary to combat erroneous biases about medication that are held by some of the patient's network.

4. Involve patients as much as possible in their own medication. It is important to get patients to be involved in decisions about their medications. Some patients may be allowed to adjust medication on their own within certain prescribed limits and some may give their own Prolixin injections.

5. Be willing to be assertive if all else fails and use whatever tactics are available. Ask patients to come into the clinic daily to take medications or even pay them to do so if needed. Once the patient experiences the benefits of an uninterrupted tenure in the community on medications, he may feel compliance is worthwhile.

Finally, Diamond concludes that although some patients may refuse medication in spite of all efforts, it is still important to maintain contact with that person and offer other kinds of assistance. Frequently, it is possible to predict crises that are likely to occur and have backup plans ready to use. Offering such services may eventually lead such patients toward accepting a trial of medication sometime in the future.

The stigma of mental illness and the pain of accepting the role of "mental patient" leads to denial of the illness and consequent avoidance of medication. Taking medication each day is a painful acknowledgment for the patient that she or he has a dreaded disease. Hence, whatever professionals and families can do to help the ill person arrive at some kind of acceptance of this existential dilemma will make a great difference in treatment compliance.

Sometimes the illness experience with its heightened sense of personal significance, for example, the extra energy of a manic episode or the desire to evade the responsibilities of a well person, may delay a person's learning to manage symptoms with medication. They may have to suffer the inevitable consequences of these high periods innumerable times before they are convinced that the price is too high.

The majority of patients have lost control over much of their lives and medication refusal may be their way of preserving some semblance of autonomy in their personal lives. Thus, it is easy for professionals and families to find themselves in a battle for control with the patient, although counterproductive to fight with her or him about medication if the likelihood of losing is there.

For families, of utmost importance is finding a clinic that persists as diligently as Diamond recommends in managing medication problems. Families can play a part, but they cannot guarantee that a patient becomes compliant with treatment. The more they know about a variety of options and are willing to try them, the more likely it is that something will eventually work.

Use and Abuse of Alcohol and Drugs

Although long recognized as a problem, the use and abuse of drugs and alcohol by persons with mental illness has not been adequately researched and addressed. This is beginning to change and practitioners need to stay alert to new recommendations for treatment. There is little useful guidance now available to families whose relative abuses drugs and alcohol.

Many young people socialize around drinking or pot smoking. People with mental illnesses have a hard time finding a social group, and if all substances are forbidden to them, they may be more excluded and alone. Anderson, Reiss, and Hogarty (1986) advise that these people cut down on use, believing that a request for total abstinence on the part of a young person trying to engage with peers may be counterproductive. Eventually, they may be helped to find social groups that do not use drugs or alcohol.

Drugs and alcohol may be a means of self-medication. Patients use them to reduce the pain of depression and anxiety or to get to sleep at night. If this is the case, better medication management may obviate the need for the other more risky substances.

Bernheim and Lehman (1985) recommend talking about the problem of drugs and alcohol as biochemical stressors and explain how they are likely to affect them. "We urge the patient to continue to discuss drug-taking behavior with us rather than deny drug use because then we can at least engender some hope into the future" (p. 82). But no patient will do this if the practitioner's attitude is condemnatory or moralistic. Bernheim and Lehman have found that an educational approach works best.

Families may find that it is very difficult to confirm the use of drugs and alcohol. Accusations only bring denials, and conflict escalates. Rather than get involved in a no-win situation, families may be wiser to concentrate on objectionable behaviors such as apathy, violence and volatile behavior, erratic and unpredictable schedules, and excessive spending, which may all be caused by substance abuse. In this way people are held accountable for the consequences of their behavior. In addition, maintaining a tight rein on money so the patient cannot buy these substances is advisable. If another family member manages the money, allowances can be reduced. This can sometimes be done by requiring the person to make a larger contribution to the family budget for rent and food.

Violence and Destruction

With the media often giving an emotionally laden and distorted picture of violence in mental illness, it is difficult to get an accurate picture of just how much violence is associated with mental illness. The general consensus at this time seems to be that there are no more incidences of criminal violence among the mentally ill than in the population in general. What is not known, however, is how much assaultive and dangerous behavior occurs in the home and never gets reported.

Swan and Lavitt (1986) undertook to fill in this gap in information through a questionnaire study of 1,156 members of the National Alliance for the Mentally Ill (NAMI). Over one-third (38%) of the sample reported that their ill relative was assaultive and destructive in the home either sometimes or frequently. When compared with nonviolent patients, violent patients were younger, less educated, more often noncompliant with medication, hospitalized more frequently, resided at home with families of less income, less frequently employed, and more often alcohol abusers. Swan found that families adjusted to these patterns of violence in a number of ways: They restricted their own behaviors, distanced themselves from their relative, asserted limits, and calmed the patient. The cost to the families was high. They experienced high levels of tension, fear, and anger, all of which generally put restrictions on their activities and markedly reduced the quality of their lives.

Practitioners aiming to help families must recognize that the circumstances that relate to patient violence may vary considerably (Bernheim & Lehman, 1985; Hatfield, 1989a). Families need to be helped to assess the violent behavior and the circumstances surrounding it. The following questions should help families to better understand the reasons for the aggression, the purposes it serves, and the factors perpetuating it:

1. Is this a real confrontation? Is there a real issue at stake? Legitimate expressions of anger might be mistaken for verbal aggressiveness or attack.

2. Is violence or threat of violence an expression of psychotic thought? Is the person under a delusion that someone is out to get her or him and that she or he must attack in self-defense, or does the patient hear voices urging her or him to do destructive things? If violence does reflect psychotic symptoms, the family cannot hope to treat the patient. They need to be sure no dangerous instruments are around and get prompt intervention through medication or hospitalization.

3. Does the person use aggression deliberately as a threatening tactic to get what she or he wants, in other words for nonpsychotic reasons, thereby taking revenge for what are considered wrongs, such as involuntary hospitalization?

4. Does aggression occur because of the patient's tenuous control under stress? Does the patient become highly agitated when she or he feels cornered or under threat? Does the patient then give signals that she or he is about to lash out?

Families are most likely called upon to actively deal with the following two kinds of aggression, and will need help from professionals to develop appropriate strategies to do so.

Deliberate Nonpsychotic Aggression

Tactics of intimidation, bullying, and revenge may become a pattern with some patients. At some point families may have to actively intervene. In another work (Hatfield, 1989a) the author recommended the following steps:

1. During a period of calm, bring family members together and plan a management strategy in detail. Decide which of the patient's demands are no longer to be tolerated. Try to anticipate how the patient will react when she or he is confronted about this behavior.

2. Convey to the patient in a calm and nonthreatening way what will not be tolerated and what the consequences will be if she or he acts aggressively. The consequences should be appropriate to the nature of the offenses. Minor acting out might bring loss of privileges, whereas assaultiveness or destroying valuable property might result in police being called and/or the person being forced to leave the home.

3. When the confrontation comes, the family must be prepared to carry out the consequences decided on. They must be carefully prepared by having other people there ready to help and emergency telephone numbers handy. When the patient is confronted, other family members should have easy access to the door in case safety becomes an issue.

4. Families will need to evaluate how well their plans worked and revise their strategies if necessary.

Losing Control

Some patients become violent not because they are trying to control others, but because they lose control over themselves. As we come to understand the tension and stress with which patients live, it is not surprising that they have a tenuous control over themselves. Nevertheless, for the sake of their families and themselves, losing control and striking out must be considered a serious matter.

1. Families need to pick up cues that their relative is beginning to lose control over her- or himself. Signs of impending aggression may vary, but common ones are increasing fearfulness, agitation,

disorganization in thinking or behavior, suspiciousness, and argu-mentativeness.

2. Other family members are urged to stay calm, for their calmness may be reassuring to the patient. Families should give the message by words or posture that they expect the patient to retain control.

3. Families are advised to give the patient physical and emo-tional space. A family member may suggest that a discussion or confrontation end temporarily until everyone has had a chance to cool off. It is probably prudent not to impose oneself physically on the patient while she or he is agitated.

4. As always, safety is of the first order. People should not stay behind closed doors with an agitated person. They must leave an avenue of escape.

5. When things are calmer, family members may want to discuss the issue with the patient and help her or him think about the potential seriousness of loss of control. The patient may need to learn to take her- or himself out of a situation when tensions are too high.

Anderson et al. (1986) recommend that caregivers ask them-selves the following questions: What kinds of situations brought on violence before? Who tends to be present? Are there particular topics that set things off? Are there particular times of the day that are stressful? Have particular medications worked in the past? Once common themes are ascertained, plans can be made to avoid the aggression.

Kanter (1984) believes that patients respond well to their fami-lies' self-protective limit setting, even if police have to be involved. Such firmness helps the patient reduce guilt feelings that could result from hurting others.

Suicidal Behavior

Few experiences are as anxiety provoking to families as living with someone who expresses suicidal thoughts or behavior. Families need to know the common warning signs of suicidal intention. Authorities in the field list the following (Bernheim & Lehman, 1985; Papolos & Papolos, 1987):

1. Expressions of personal worthlessness or concerns about having committed an unpardonable sin.
2. Expressions of hopelessness about the future.

3. Preoccupation with morbid thoughts of death.
4. The presence of hallucinatory voices that instruct the person to hurt or kill her- or himself.
5. Increased risk-taking behavior (e.g., driving too fast, drinking heavily, handling knives or guns).
6. A sudden, unexplainable brightening of mood in a person who has been chronically depressed.
7. Indications that the patient is getting her or his affairs in order (e.g., writing a will, patching up old disputes, giving prized possessions away).
8. Discussions of concrete, specific suicidal plans.

If relatives even suspect that their relative is contemplating suicide, they should call the treating psychiatrist immediately. The myth that people who threaten suicide never do so is a dangerous one to subscribe to. If the family suspects suicidal potential, Papolos and Papolos (1987) recommend the following:

> Remove access to guns, knives, medications, automobiles, and other potentially lethal instruments.
> Monitor the taking of medications to guard against overdose.
> Let the patient talk about suicidal thoughts without the expression of shock or condemnation. Conveying the knowledge that suicidal thoughts are not unusual in severe depression may allow the person to feel less guilty and isolated.

Bernheim and Lehman (1985) advise families not to try to argue patients out of suicidal ideas. Such behavior may only make the patient more adamant about persisting in these thoughts. Angry responses may further promote the patient's sense of being alienated and misunderstood. They suggest that family members lend an empathic ear to the patient's concerns and be clear about the limits of their ability to prevent suicide. They provide the following model of what the family might say:

> I know that you are hurting and that things need to change for you. We all love you very much, need you, and would feel very bad if you were to die. I am glad that you were able to tell me how bad you feel so that together we can get you some help. I'm concerned that we cannot stop you from hurting yourself if you are determined to do so, and we need to go see your doctor now to get some additional help. (p. 117)

If there is even a remote possibility that a patient may become suicidal, families may want to have some carefully developed plans made long before they are needed. The following are some questions families should ask beforehand. At what point should they restrict the use of the automobile? When should they seek outside help and from whom? Should they call the ambulance or police to transport the person to the hospital? (Bernheim & Lehman, 1985).

Finally, however, families must come to terms with the fact that living with a mentally ill person often involves some risk of suicide. Constant monitoring will not necessarily guarantee a patient's safety. Suicide is sometimes an impulsive act that neither professionals nor families can prevent. Excessive vigilance may only lead to aggravation, overprotection, and family burnout. However difficult it may be, some balance must be sought.

Manic Behavior

Coping with a relative manifesting manic behavior can be exhausting and demoralizing. The patient has boundless energy and may make rash and impulsive decisions that impact on other family members, without having the capacity for taking responsibility for these acts. Huge debts may pile up and the legal system may hold the patient's family accountable. Individuals may become intrusive and demanding, harass others, violate social and sexual mores, and/or get into trouble with the law (Papolos & Papolos, 1987).

Some manic persons become exceedingly hostile and angry. The fear that the ill person will lose control leads families to attempt to placate their relative, a solution that usually does not succeed. Mania, say Papolos and Papolos (1987), continues long after the family's stamina and patience is exhausted. Manic episodes rarely end safely without hospitalization. A manic person, however, may not go along with such plans without a struggle.

While authorities in the field are able to offer helpful suggestions to families struggling with problems of depression and other disturbing behaviors, they have been able to offer little help to families facing a manic relative. This is understandable because so little is known, but it must be remembered that families may be subjected to the chaotic state of their relative for some time before hospitalization is possible.

When faced with these volatile personalities, logic suggests that families stay as low-keyed as possible, abnormally low-keyed to handle the stress of the situation. Requests to the patient should be made calmly and firmly, without long explanations, accusations, or arguments. All members need to pull together to maintain a firm, strong counterforce against the patient's erratic behaviors. Families may need to find ways to spell each other, for even a few hours of manic behavior can be exhausting. Members may need to take turns in getting sleep or respite from daily problems until professional care can be utilized.

In the meantime, families can try to prevent as many disastrous consequences of manic behavior as possible. They can take control of car keys, money, and charge plates. Valuable household things and jewelry can be locked away lest they be sold or given away, bank accounts closed if possible, and costly long-distance calls made unavailable through locking the telephone. The family can also review what happened in former episodes of mania to develop preventive strategies for the current one.

Finally, of course, the family will need to pull out all stops in order to get the patient into treatment. They will need to consider what is available in the community: Is there a crisis team that would come out? Can the police be involved in a helpful way? How will they proceed if the patient's aberrant behavior gets her or him arrested?

These suggestions are offered with some humility, for we know how out-of-bounds a manic person can be, and how few things seem to penetrate the person in a full-blown manic episode.

Emergency Treatment

Many families are required to live weeks or even months with a seriously disoriented person before legal steps can be instituted to require hospitalization. Families have great difficulty understanding a system that will allow a person to live in a bizarre and undignified manner, inadvertently destroying the few relationships that she or he has, carelessly losing and wasting property, and alienating and exhausting those who try to care for her or him. One of the most painful experiences a family can have is to stand by helplessly as its relative daily becomes more dysfunctional and do nothing about it. Although laws vary from state to state, in most states dangerousness to self or others are the only criteria for involuntary treatment. Some states have such expanded criteria as inability to care for self or evidence of grave disability.

Families need a great deal of support during what seems like an interminable period until they can get help for their relative.

Once involuntary treatment becomes a possibility, families need to understand the procedures that pertain to their particular state. What the state law is regarding involuntary commitment and how it is initiated needs to be a part of all classes and workshops for families. Most families will need this kind of information at some point.

Even though families may welcome the possibility that their relative will finally get treatment, they loathe the commitment process. Families worry that fear and resentment will prevail, that their relative will never forgive them, and that the relationship will be permanently destroyed.

Vine (1982, p. 38) describes the feelings of a daughter when she was required to provide evidence that her mother needed hospitalization. "I felt like I was turning state's evidence," the daughter said as she described how her mother did not sleep for two nights, tried to run away, cried and screamed in her room, and threatened to have the local newspaper investigate her husband and child. "It was as if my mother were sitting there and I were sending her to jail," she said. She could not believe that she was sitting there and citing one crazy act after another to prove her mother's incompetence—the mismatched clothes, the mess in the house, the frequent car trips when nobody knew where she was. Finally, there was the heartbreaking accusation of the mother: "Maggie, how can you do this to me?"

While resentment, anger, and mistrust may permeate the air for a long period of time, the strain in relationships usually abates over time. Sometimes patients are grateful to their families for this act of caring and a few may actually say so. In any case, families may take some consolation in the fact that they managed to protect someone unable to take responsibility for her- or himself.

Summary

Mental illness in the family means that crises are frequent. Families can understandably be overwhelmed by such devastating problems as assaultiveness, suicide attempts, manic episodes, and treatment refusal. They expect help from professionals in solving these problems. Professionals can teach families how to anticipate these crises and the most effective management techniques to use. They can also help them locate appropriate community resources and provide support and guidance until the crisis is over.

CHAPTER 10

Planning for the Long Range

Once the more acute problems abate, families must prepare themselves for the long-term aspects of the mental illness: How can they best help their relative rebuild her or his life and what community resources are available for this purpose? How can the financial resources and energies of family members be most fairly distributed so that the needs of everyone in the family are balanced? To what extent does the family need to alter its goals and aspirations in order to accommodate the disabled member's needs?

The Family's Role in Rehabilitation

If the patient lives at home or is in frequent contact with the family, it can play an important role in rehabilitation. Those who have been ill for a long time undoubtedly missed many opportunities for learning social skills, hence the family may be helpful in the process of learning or re-learning what was missed. This does not mean hovering over the disabled person or constantly nagging, but in the course of day-to-day life the patient's deficiencies may be kept in mind so that ordinary daily activities can be used as sources of learning.

Identifying Strengths and Weaknesses

For those who remain significantly disabled, who are withdrawn and prefer considerably restricted lives, the first consideration is to find an avenue out of such an impoverished existence. Families may recall earlier interests the patient enjoyed and try to re-establish them or try to open new avenues of interest—any interests that will connect the mentally ill person to the world again. Almost any stimulus has the potential for opening a door, whetting an interest, or beginning the slow process of rebuilding skills and encouraging participation in the world.

A well-known educational principle is that a person should build from strengths. Families need to gradually encourage their relative to take responsibility for ongoing family life. She or he needs to feel like a contributing member, and should be expected to perform at her or his best. That means determining the patient's strengths and what she or he enjoys doing most so as to assign those tasks first. Unless the patient is required to do what she or he can do, other family members may feel exploited and resentful.

Motivating the Patient

The issue of motivation will surely arise when working with families. Families are baffled and frustrated at their relative's lack of drive, lethargy, and general disinterest in the surrounding world. Researchers now generally agree that this pattern of low motivation, along with affective blunting and poverty of speech is an inherent part of some schizophrenic disorders (Andreasen, 1984). These behaviors are not alleviated by neuroleptic medications and may sometimes be aggravated by them. Thus, psychosocial treatments appear to be the most effective treatment for countering these negative symptoms.

If families have the patience and persistence and are careful not to overstimulate the patient, they may be instrumental in helping their relative overcome some of these deficits. The energy and persistence required, however, should not be underestimated.

Another explanation for low motivation is the high levels of anxiety with which many mentally ill people live. The world of the mentally ill often seems dangerous and frightening, and efforts on their part to reach out, to try something new, bring on intolerable levels of anxiety. Left without the encouragement, support, and assistance of caring people, the afflicted people are in a state of constant avoidance and retreat. Families can help by learning the fine art of gently nudging their relative into new activity, taking a few small steps at a time.

Lack of self-confidence and self-esteem also plays a part in low motivation. Patients lose faith in their own competence when they try to compete and meet social expectations against the odds presented by their impairments. Frequent failure coupled with social rejection leads to profound discouragement and reluctance to try again. Families can make a difference in the slow repair of self-esteem and restoration of confidence.

Promoting Independent Living Skills

How far each patient can go in becoming fully independent cannot be predicted. Ability to live independently depends upon the ability to budget and manage money, maintain acceptable appearance and personal hygiene, keep surroundings safe and clean, and manage shopping and cooking. The daily activities of most households provide opportunities to practice these skills. Family educators can guide families in using problem-solving approaches helpful in their efforts at guiding their relative. (Chapter 12 discusses teaching problem-solving skills to families.)

Psychiatrically disabled people are often lonely and bored because they have trouble establishing a social life for themselves. They may have difficulty taking on the appropriate social role for a given situation; they may be unable to put themselves in the place of another; and they may fail to recognize a sense of mutual obligation in social situations. Families and caring professionals can be helpful in interpreting the more subtle aspects of social behavior and in encouraging the patient to develop greater social competence.

While families can be helpful in rehabilitation, they cannot be expected to do it alone. They need the help of a wide array of community resources. Family educators in any locality must be fully prepared to know the available community resources, their particular philosophy or style of working, and how they can be accessed.

Community Treatment Resources

As the patient begins making a transition to a more peer-oriented society, thought must be given as to how that transition can be made in a way that stresses the patient as little as possible. Only one change should be made at a time. Priorities should be based on the transitions that are easiest for the patient to make or those changes most needed for the family's well-being.

Psychiatric Rehabilitation

Individuals with a chronic psychiatric illness have varying types and levels of disability. Psychiatric rehabilitation is based on the assumption that these disabilities can be modified or overcome through appropriate training. The overall goal of psychiatric rehabilitation, according to leaders in the field, is to assure that the disabled person can perform those physical, emotional, social, and intellectual skills necessary for living and working in the community (Anthony & Liberman, 1987).

Psychosocial rehabilitation centers have increased in numbers in the past decade. The settings may vary, but Anthony and Liberman believe that they should emphasize the following:

1. Strategies that help people to *cope* with their environment rather than *succumb* to it.
2. Health induction rather than symptom reduction.
3. Belief in the potential productivity of the most severely disabled.

SKILLS TRAINING

Central to most rehabilitation centers is a preplanned series of experiences to help the disabled persons gain or re-gain important social skills. They are taught problem-solving skills, interpersonal-communication skills, and strategies for dealing with environmental stress. The psychiatric disorders with the greatest chronicity—schizophrenia, major depression, and organic syndromes—are the ones that require the most skills training. While medications significantly reduce symptoms, some people do not respond to medications and others persist in having their symptoms despite optimum medication adjustment. As we noted earlier, the negative or deficit symptoms of schizophrenia do not respond well to medication. Psychosocial rehabilitation is now the best hope for remediating these deficiencies.

SUPPORTIVE INTERVENTIONS

For many people with severe disabilities, full restoration of social and vocational skills is not likely. What are needed then are strategies aimed at helping the individual compensate for the disability. Anthony and Liberman (1987) recommend (1) locating living, learning, and working environments that can accommodate these residual deficits, and (2) helping the individual and her or his family adjust their expectations to meet those that are realistically attainable.

A supportive person may reduce the effects of the person's disability through the role of friend, companion, advocate, or advisor. Supportive environments such as sheltered workshops and highly supervised living environments, as distinguished from skill-development interventions, focus less on systematic and direct change of the patient's behavior, and focus more on supporting and accommodating the patient's present level of functioning (Anthony & Liberman, 1987).

In the search for the appropriate fit of patient to rehabilitation service, many questions need to be asked about the patient's personality, lifestyle, interests, and preferences, as well as her or his deficits and symptoms. It is frequently noted by the families in the National Alliance for the Mentally Ill (NAMI) movement that their relatives reject the programs in their communities. Patients claim that these programs get boring, that they are not compatible in age and functionality with other clients, and that their goals are not achieved in these programs. While some of these comments may reflect the generally negative and resistant patterns associated with mental illness, it is probably true that we need an influx of new creative ideas and programs based on a more empathic understanding of people with mental illnesses.

Families may find psychosocial programs in hospitals, psychiatric day centers, psychosocial rehabilitation centers, and community mental health centers. They vary in structure, expectancies, and comprehensiveness. Family educators should help families locate available resources and evaluate their appropriateness for their family member. Questions to ask are: What is the nature and comprehensiveness of the programs? What are their objectives? To what extent and how do they measure outcomes to determine if objectives are met? What are the levels of expectation and how much is the program individualized for each person? How well trained and experienced is the staff? What relationship do they have to medical personnel and medication management? What kinds of attitudes do they have toward families?

Residential Programs

Social planners who assume that families can be the primary source of care for their mentally ill relative are truly misguided. The time soon comes when most families realize that they can no longer tolerate the stresses of having their relative live at home. When a family arrives at such a decision, professional helpers should support them in their stand and facilitate the patient's move to another facility as soon as possible. They should never criticize the family for this decision nor create guilt by implying that they are rejecting or abandoning their relative (Anderson, Reiss, & Hogarty, 1986).

Even when the patient is doing relatively well at home, the family and/or patient may feel it is time to separate. Howe (1985), former president of NAMI, probably reflects the views of the NAMI membership when he argues that for families care means 168 hours of duty per week (as contrasted to providers' usual 40-hour week) and that families do not have the option of burnout. Howe points out that out-of-home providers can be more objective in setting and enforcing rules than can families and that they have (or should have) special training in dealing with the mentally ill. In our society, it is normal for adult children to move out of parental homes and live among peers, but often not an option for the mentally ill. We value independence in this country. And "Trying to encourage independence in a setting (the home) that has symbolized one's dependency since infancy," Howe states, "is doing it the hard way" (p. 17).

Community residential services have been an area of some expansion in the past decade, but there is still not nearly enough housing nor the variety that is needed to insure appropriate care for all who need it. There are no scientifically validated models that are best for everyone. We do not know which types of patients flourish in which kinds of settings. This leaves consumers, families, and case managers on their own to figure out what is best for a given patient—assuming that there is any choice at all.

Residences are best in which staff understand the necessity of being responsive to the perceptual, cognitive, and emotional vulnerabilities caused by mental illness. There needs to be a fine balance between overcontrolling and overprotecting patients and not offering enough support and exceeding the demands of a patient's capabilities. For some patients the line between the two excesses is very narrow.

There are many issues still to be resolved regarding what is the most desirable setting for many patients: Should residences be conceptualized as treatment centers or living quarters? Should staff be professional or lay? How much supervision should be given? How close a connection should they have to mental health centers? Should the housing be considered transitional or long term? (Cournos, 1987).

Segal, Everett-Dille, and Moyles (1979) studied 499 residents and 234 home operators to determine if agreement between residents and operators on the nature of the home environment would predict good outcome. It turned out that the best predictors of good outcomes were the perceptions of the residents themselves. Those who were satisfied with the home and experienced it as a self-contained facility that was not treatment-oriented had the best outcome. Other studies cited by Cournos (1987) supported the idea that good outcome correlated with the patient's perception that the home was a good match for her or his needs. Perceptions of staff were only weakly correlated with successful outcome.

When families are involved in the community placement of their relative, there are many things to consider. First of all, of course, they must assess their relative's needs. How much supervision does she or he need? What kind of people (age, sex, culture) does she or he adjust to best? Is the patient able to monitor her or his own medications and remember her or his own appointments? Does the patient know budgeting, food preparation, and cleaning or will she or he need to be taught all of these? How vulnerable is she or he to stress? Such an assessment leads to a search for the best fit between the patient and available resources. Sadly, most patients still have to settle for much less than the optimal situation for their needs.

Vocational Rehabilitation

Our culture places great value on work. It is not surprising, then, that the issue of work looms large in the concerns of most families and that it is not an easy one to resolve. Many severely mentally ill people have a diminished capacity to work. So much energy goes into struggling with their symptoms that there is little left for anything else. The thought of work for some mentally ill people produces high anxiety for they see themselves as at risk for another failure. The stigma against mental illness is such that employers tend not to give favorable consideration to applicants who have these disorders. Anthony and Liberman (1987) report that unemployment among the chronic mentally ill is as high as 70%. Employment rates following hospital discharge, they report, range between 10–30%, and only 10–15% sustain employment 1 to 5 years later. The authors point to deficits in work tolerance, endurance, following instructions, problem solving, task orientations, concentration, and ability to accept criticism, as factors that get in the way of successful employment.

Nevertheless, work is considered an important aspect of treatment, many clients say they want to work, and families tend to expect it. Clients experience enhanced self-esteem from seeing themselves as productive and contributing members of society. It gives them a reason for getting up in the morning, and it provides them with a structured day. Work is a normative experience in our society, and we need to encourage a deeper commitment to helping those who can work to develop the skills and the supportive environment in which to do so.

There are few data available to indicate which client characteristics predict future success in work. There may not be a high correlation between vocational success, degree of symptomatology, and/or general social functioning. Marrone, Horgan, Scripture, and Grossman (1984) synthesized what is known about mental illness and work, and concluded that some of the factors that are associated with successful vocational rehabilitation are:

- A work history.
- A value of work to the client that she or he can express.
- A course of illness that is relatively predictable.
- A cooperative approach to mental health treatment.
- Past, consistent participation in a structured program.
- An ability to make a good impression both physically and verbally.
- The support from others of vocational rehabilitation involvement.
- A stable living situation.

Vocational rehabilitation may take place in a number of ways. Families and patients need to consider the options available in their community. Possibilities to be explored are:

1. *Sheltered workshops.* The sheltered workshop is a simulated work environment that emphasizes job-appropriate work skills and work habits. A high level of support is usually given to help the client deal with stress.

2. *Transitional employment programs* (TEPs). In a temporary job placement, clients are placed with an employer who has agreed to commit certain positions at usual wages to clients of an agency. The agency provides on-site support, guidance, and supervision of the client on the job. The agency providers later facilitate placement in competitive jobs or in vocational rehabilitation. Foundations for this kind of service were laid in Fountain House, established in New York City in the 1940s. These programs are probably indicated for people who need help in developing confidence, who

have difficulty keeping a job, and who need to begin getting work references.

3. *Volunteer work.* A placement with a volunteer agency may be useful when finances are not a major problem, when the individual does not have enough energy to commit to a TEP, or when the individual has a high level of talent or intellectual capacity that may make usual TEP placements intolerable.

4. *Supported work.* A relatively new concept undergoing trial and much scrutiny is that of supported work where clients are placed in usual kinds of employment and given considerable support. Arguments in favor of this approach are: It is "real work" as opposed to a simulated situation; therefore, it is less demeaning for some than a sheltered workshop. It is considered permanent rather than temporary so the client does not need to worry about making another transition soon. Those who favor supported work say that the way to learn to work is to take a job; intermediate steps of temporary work and work adjustment training do not help enough to warrant their use.

There is a Division of Vocational Rehabilitation Services in every state, and local offices are located in most communities. Mentally ill people are entitled to vocational rehabilitation services if they have a degree of disability that interferes with their ability to pursue gainful employment. They must have a reasonable chance of being able to perform in a suitable occupation. Vocational Rehabilitation Services provides evaluation, counseling, and training to disabled people. Programs are funded by federal and state dollars.

Anderson and colleagues (1986) caution schizophrenic patients and families not to move too quickly into the work arena. They believe that there are significant risks associated with training and employment that precipitate relapse, and a significant chance that attempts to return to work will result in failure. Anderson et al. state that most patients need at least 10 to 12 months of recuperative time after an acute episode before they can begin steps toward training or work. They advocate that the patient first show increased capacity to do jobs around the home that involve such things as getting up on a regular schedule, maintaining routine, and completing sizable tasks.

The ideal vocational program, according to Anderson et al., would incorporate the following factors:

- A slow and gradual assumption of work responsibilities.
- Low levels of involvement with co-workers.

- Close supervision from a supportive supervisor.
- Moderately interesting, but not excessively complex, work.

While few jobs meet the above requirements, the list can help families begin to consider kinds of work appropriate to their relative's abilities. Transition even to part-time work or school can be a big hurdle for a person with a severe impairment. Small steps are recommended and not too many changes in the person's life should be attempted at any one time.

Case Management

Patients must use a number of local, state, and federal agencies, as well as private organizations, to have their needs met for housing, social and vocational rehabilitation, medication, income, and treatment. Typically these services are fragmented, uncoordinated, and unresponsive. Patients with severe mental illnesses have great difficulty negotiating these complex systems. Hence, there has developed in many places a new kind of mental health worker whose job it is to coordinate and monitor services.

At issue is whether case management services should be the function of the major treatment provider or whether they should be a separate function. Lamb (1982) and Kanter (1985) tend to agree that the case manager should be more than a broker of services, hence they believe that case management should come from the professional who has the primary relationship with the patient. In their opinion, that person is the one who understands the patient best, maintains a close relationship with her or him, and can maintain a continuity that is not possible if another layer of bureaucracy is created.

In any case, it is generally agreed that the case management function is an important one and that it requires knowledge of the psychopathology of mental illness, as well as considerable skill in dealing with difficult individuals and poorly organized community systems.

Intagliata, Willer, and Egri (1986) believe that family members have a major contribution to make in identifying the needs of their mentally ill relative. They are an important source of information with regard to their relative's history of illness, treatment, and current functioning. Families are important in supporting and encouraging their relative in the program created for her or him and in monitoring her or his progress.

Financial Resources

It has been estimated that only about 25% of those with schizophrenia are self-supporting. The largest source of income for the remainder is Supplementary Social Security (SSI), a federal program with supplements provided by some states. Applications for this program are made through the Social Security Office. The person's income and assets are considered in determining eligibility. If the person is denied benefits, she or he has the right to appeal. Eligibility for SSI may help establish eligibility for other kinds of programs such as Medicaid, food stamps, and some rental and housing assistance (Torrey, 1983).

Social Security Disability Insurance (SSDI) may be available to those who worked prior to their illnesses, or to children of a parent retired on social security benefits when it can be established that they were disabled before the age of 22.

Food stamps are another supplementary source of support to low-income, disabled people. Medicaid and Medicare are the two programs created to help the elderly, indigent, and disabled. Medicaid is run by the states, with benefits varying considerably from state to state. Medicare, a federal program for the aged and disabled, covers most in-patient and some out-patient services (Torrey, 1983).

Family educators must be thoroughly familiar with all entitlement programs. They should set aside a significant block of time in each class or workshop to explain these programs to families. They cannot take for granted that families will be told these things as their relative goes through other parts of the system.

Concluding Thoughts

Mentally ill people have the full range of human needs. Besides food and shelter, they need social life, crisis care, and recreation. Resources available to the mentally ill vary considerably from place to place. The family educator must be in a position to identify all resources, know the rules of eligibility, and how one accesses them.

Balancing Family Needs

Even when they take full advantage of what society has to offer the mentally ill, families usually find that there are still considerable demands on their own time, energy, and money. Typically, in the beginning, families spare nothing in their efforts to get their relative well. In their early desperation, they may spend huge amounts of money at expensive treatment centers with little consideration for the long-range financial needs of the total family. All time and energy may be focused on the ill person with little awareness that others in the family feel neglected. Family educators can be helpful by urging families to sit down and begin planning for the long-range needs of all members. Families need to be reminded that their resources are finite and that the mental illness may last a very long time.

Franks (1987) gathered data from 408 families of the Alliance for the Mentally Ill of Massachusetts on the economic contributions made by families to their mentally ill member. She found that the amount of money spent ranged from 0 to almost $23,000 per year, with a mean dollar expenditure of $3,311 per year, with most of it going for food, shelter, and other support costs. Her assessment of time spent caring for the ill person revealed that the range was from 0 to 792 hours per year. Franks's study gives some idea of the temporal demands made upon a family, as well as the variability in expenditures that families make.

Family members should be encouraged to sit down together and estimate how much income they can reasonably expect to earn in their lifetimes, what assets they now have, and what the major needs of all family members will be. To be considered are college education costs of young people in the family, retirement needs and potential health and long-term care needs of older members, as well as the special costs that mental illness poses for the family. There is no alternative but to try to balance these needs in the best way possible.

A very special source of anxiety for most families is who will look after the disabled member when the rest of the family is gone. When families have some money to leave, they are advised to consider very carefully how this money will be left so that their ill relative profits maximally and does not lose entitlements. Families need to work out carefully with their lawyer a trust arrangement suitable to protecting the disabled member. Through affiliates of NAMI in many states, families may be able to purchase a service that is a type of surrogate parent—for example, Planned Lifetime Assistance Network (PLAN) of Maryland—which can be paid for after they are gone through a trust arrangement.

Medical insurance is another area families need to consider early on, so that in the case of their absence their ill relative will still be covered and will be able to use her or his insurance as wisely as possible. If the ill person was under 19 at onset, she or he may be eligible to remain on the family policy as long as she or he lives at home and is a dependent. It is important to know exactly what the policy covers: What percentage of in-patient and out-patient costs does it cover? Are there limits on the number of days per year? Is there a maximum total lifetime benefit for mental illness? Families are urged to read their policies carefully and ask questions at the subscriber's personnel office. Families will need to estimate their relative's long-term medical needs as they make ongoing decisions about the use of their insurance. Not only must they be temperate in the use of insurance, they must also be careful that physicians do not recommend excessively expensive treatments. Finally, in the name of cost consciousness they must learn to read hospital and psychiatry bills to be sure that they have not been charged for a service that they did not receive. They need to question their bills and bring discrepancies to the attention of those who did the billing and to their insurance carriers.

Summary

Because of the long-term nature of mental illness and the desire of families that their disabled member have the best possible life in spite of the disorder, family educators should help families to identify the resources that society has provided for this population and then help families decide what, in addition, they may be able to contribute to their relative's growth and rehabilitation. Educators should help families see the long-range picture and help them plan their resources to balance the needs of all of the members of the family.

III

Educational Approaches

CHAPTER 11

Learning and Instruction

In Section II of this book, we have identified a wide range of information, knowledge, and skills that families need to cope effectively with a mentally ill relative. In this chapter, we explore the ways in which this learning can be accomplished in the most efficient and cost effective way. Issues of efficiency and cost are often not attended to when new programs for families are conceived, even though agencies are increasingly required to justify programs on that basis. In this period of fiscal restraint, one program's costs reduces resources available to others. Providers must learn to justify the rigors of their programs in terms of time and program outcome, and they must be able to show how their programs compare with rival training practices.

Families of the mentally ill have limited time and energy to pursue educational activities for themselves. The demands related to the mental illness are high, these families have all the usual responsibilities to other members, and they have to work for a living and manage their affairs. Families must sometimes feel a little cynical when they are urged to participate in lengthy therapy or psychoeducational programs and at the same time are told to put more distance between themselves and their relative and to go on with their own lives. Experts in adult education find that the adult learners, in general, say that efficiency is an important criterion of a successful program (Tough, 1979). The participants Tough studied wanted programs that provided the easiest, fastest, and cheapest way to learn.

Efficiency in learning involves: (1) accurately learning the most amount of information in the least amount of time, (2) retaining this material over an extended period of time, and (3) broadly generalizing these learnings to other life situations. Learning theorists and educational psychologists have researched the foundations of such learning extensively. From their findings, we will present the most important guidelines for learning and instruction in work with families.

Principles of Learning

Learning has been defined in various ways, but for our present purposes, we will assume learning to be a growth in competence that comes from the acquisition of new skills, attitudes, and knowledge. A discussion of attitudes and skills is delayed until the next chapter. Our focus in this chapter is on the acquisition of new knowledge, or cognitive learning.

Cognitive learning does not imply that the learner is a passive receptacle to be filled up; rather, we believe that learning is an active and dynamic process. The learner is an active information processor, and what matters is how the new material is perceived and how it becomes organized and stored in the learner's mind. Perception and organization are two interrelated processes with no two people processing information exactly the same. Teachers do not achieve the desired learning objectives directly, but they can be vital in facilitating the process. The learner, of course, controls the final outcome.

Skillful instruction requires an understanding of: (1) the ways in which people are motivated to learn, (2) the determinants of long-term retention of knowledge, and (3) the extent to which application of knowledge or transfer of learning takes place.

Motivation to Learn

Motivation concerns the "why" of behavior. It cannot be directly observed, but rather must be inferred by observing the direction, intensity, and consistency of behavior over time. We use motivation concepts to explain what initiates or energizes learning (Hudgins et al., 1983). While school children may be motivated by praise, grades, or avoidance of censure, these factors play little or no role in adult learning. Most adults, Cross (1981) found in her review of research on adult motivation, give practical reasons for learning.

Families of the mentally ill express many pragmatic reasons for wanting to learn about mental illness. Obviously, when families freely choose to attend workshops and classes, the motivation for learning is there. They want to overcome their sense of helplessness and become competent in meeting the unusual demands created by mental illness. Hence, the educational leader should face no problems in motivating class participants. Leaders need only identify interests already there and then build programs to respond to these interests.

Providers are cautioned not to readily assume that they know the needs of families. As we have noted in Chapter 3, professionals do not always infer family need correctly from clinical observation. Providers may sensitize themselves to family need in a number of ways. Books written by families, many of which have already been mentioned in this book, can enhance the process of understanding (e.g., see Vine, 1982; Walsh, 1985; Wasow, 1982; Wechsler, Wechsler, & Karpf, 1972). Family educators can also profit from empathic professional writing (e.g., see Anderson, Reiss, & Hogarty, 1986; Bernheim & Lehman, 1985; Hatfield & Lefley, 1987; Torrey, 1983).

Some providers have tried to motivate families by promising more by way of patient improvement (or even cure) than they could possibly have delivered. The credibility of the entire profession suffers when such tactics are used. Other providers have tried to induce fear in the family as to the terrible things that could happen to their relative if the provider's treatment was not used. Some arouse further anxiety and guilt by implying that the family wants to keep their relative sick and dependent on them and that is why it refuses the service being urged upon it. Such tactics border on the unethical, and are definitely not recommended. Those who understand families and have the talent to develop programs to meet these needs find that families do respond.

Some providers rely heavily on their personal enthusiasm to "sell" families on the advantages of their programs. Enthusiasm and enjoyment of teaching families is a necessary but insufficient motivator for learning. Adult learners, in particular, look for real substance in what is taught. They have a concept of themselves as capable of making their own decisions, as well as a deep need to do so. They resist and resent situations in which others impose their will on them (Knowles, 1984).

Long-Term Retention of Knowledge

While the degree of learner motivation has a strong influence on learner retention, attention to other factors is also necessary. Research in learning theory has shown that facts, information, and illustrative data are stored by learners with differential success

(Ausubel, 1968; Good & Brophy, 1977; Hudgins et al., 1983). If new material is learned in isolation from what is already known, even substantive passages may not be retained. The person's prior knowledge and the way new material is organized and presented is of prime importance.

The theoretical formulations of Ausubel (1963) are especially useful in helping us understand how learning retention takes place. Ausubel believes that didactic teaching is the simplest and most efficient approach to learning and that the teacher's primary role is the transmission of knowledge. Educational work with families usually involves some didactic teaching and some skills development. The work of Ausubel will serve as a foundation for discussion of didactic teaching.

To understand Ausubel's theory, one must understand his concept of cognitive structure—cognitive structure refers to the organization of ideas about a subject matter that the learner already possesses. Knowledge, according to this model, is normally hierarchically organized, with more specific items of information subordinated to higher order concepts and generalizations. The comprehensiveness, accuracy, and adequacy of this organization all play major roles in facilitating the acquisition and retention of new material. Good organization provides cognitive hooks upon which to hang new information.

Cognitive structure is Ausubel's model of long-term memory. New information is not stored in long-term memory randomly, but rather is stored systematically and in hierarchical order. To enhance this storage process, information must be presented in an appropriately organized way (Ausubel, 1968; Hudgins et al., 1983). From this model of learning, some guidelines to instruction emerge.

1. Instructors must understand the level of organization (i.e., cognitive structure) that the learner already possesses; for, to be meaningful and to be remembered, the new information must relate to what the learner already knows. Isolated answers and bits of unrelated information are not meaningful and will not be efficiently retained.

2. The instructor must clearly present the key concepts to be learned, and should keep that number to a minimum. The concepts that any individual can fully comprehend in a session are really very few, and there is no point in exceeding the pace of learning beyond that which learners can grasp and integrate into their existing knowledge. A common mistake of inexperienced teachers is to try to "cover" too much and to fail to help the learner to differentiate between the key ideas and related and supporting

information of lesser importance. As a result, the learner becomes confused and learning time is inefficient and wasted.

To reiterate, to be appropriately retained in long-term memory, the number of key concepts must be kept few in number and presented with great clarity. Many examples must be used so that these concepts are as comprehensive and stable as possible.

3. If people tend to store information in well-patterned ways, as Ausubel insists, it then follows that new knowledge should be presented to learners in carefully sequenced ways. Usually more general and inclusive material should precede more detailed information. The general information will serve as a structure for anchoring the more specific ideas. Haphazardly presented information will be poorly understood and easily forgotten.

To illustrate the points already made, let us take the concept, typically taught to families, that highly stimulating environments are stressful to patients with schizophrenia. This is a key concept with considerable usefulness for families. Our first concern is for the background of information these families already have to which the new concept can be related. While families may know from their own experience that their relative is vulnerable to stress, they cannot fully understand the phenomenon without having some organized background information about brain functioning and the cognitive deficits of schizophrenic patients. The key concept of stress vulnerability must be related to this information for it to have meaning. In addition, the key concept must be explained with great clarity and many examples must be used to expand and enrich the meaning. Learners should be actively engaged in discussion and involved in identifying the many kinds of stressors that occur in typical environments. The important points to be carried away from the session, however, are not the specific instances of stress that are identified, but rather a comprehensive and well-stabilized understanding of stimulation as a factor in patient stress. When the key concept is thoroughly taught, the individual can later identify specific instances whenever they occur.

This discussion raises questions about the learning that might take place in settings in which the primary approach is answering questions in response to specific problems that are raised. Are these more isolated bits of information likely to be remembered? Certainly, providing information at the specific instance in which it is asked induces a strong motivation for it to be learned. We are instinctively disinclined to delay responding to a question that has an immediacy for that individual. Yet, if learning theorists are correct, this kind of learning is less likely to be organized into a comprehensive body of knowledge and, is, therefore less likely to be retained over a long period of time. In order for families to develop an organized field of knowledge, professionals in these situations might recommend books to them or classes/workshops if available, or they might organize classes themselves. Once families have a background from which to draw, professionals need to be sure that they relate each answer given to this broader base of knowledge.

Transfer of Learning

Our final concern in providing effective education to families is how to teach so that learning can be applied to the solution of new problems in life situations. This is an issue of transfer of learning. There is much practical interest in how widely and accurately information learned in a formal setting will be applied in other settings. While some transfer of learning probably goes on whenever one learns something, the efficiency and effectiveness of transfer can be enhanced if we deliberately teach with that purpose in mind (Bigge & Hunt, 1962; Ellis, 1965).

Transferability of learning, Ausubel (1968) believes, is largely a function of the relevance, meaningfulness, clarity, stability, integrativeness, and explanatory power of the originally learned material. To use Ausubel's concepts, learning will transfer to the extent that cognitive structure is effectively organized and reorganized. Other authors (Bigge & Hunt, 1962; Ellis, 1965; Hudgins et al., 1983) say that further steps should be taken to insure that transfer of learning takes place.

USING A VARIETY OF EXAMPLES
IN THE LEARNING SITUATION

The transferability of learning depends on the extent to which the learning situation illustrates how to apply the new concept in as many specific contexts as possible. If the teacher provides a substantial number of illustrations, the learner will begin to identify the specific contexts in her or his home environment to which the concept can be applied. In teaching, both similarities and differences in contexts should be stressed; such examples are particularly valuable where confusion by learners is likely.

In the example we used earlier about schizophrenic patients' vulnerability to stress, the instructor may point out a variety of instances of stress—too many people, confusion and noise, complicated communication, unexpected events, strange places, and the like. Class participants should be engaged in identifying stressful situations in their relative's experiences. It should be noted that a wide variety of factors can be stressful to the vulnerable individual.

DEVELOPING GENERALIZATIONS

Once learners have been exposed to several contexts, they can be helped to find the common elements in them. Then the relationships between the common elements can be shown. From these relationships a "generalization" can develop, sometimes referred to as a principle or a rule. These principles or generalizations can then be stored in long-term memory; they have the potential for being valid in future situations. "People with schizophrenia are vulnerable to stress" is a generalization or principle. It may be arrived at inductively from a variety of examples, or the idea may be presented with many illustrations to clarify it. Typically in adult learners we present the generalization, develop many instances, and return again to the statement of generalization. It is the generalization, of course, that learners carry with them from the learning situation and which becomes a part of their cognitive structure. To insure transfer to new situations, the teacher demonstrates to the learner the applicability of the new principle in increasingly varied and complex situations.

IDENTIFYING TASK SIMILARITY

The likelihood that learning will transfer from the learning situation to a life situation depends on the perceived similarity between the two situations. Effective teachers do not leave to chance that this transfer will occur; rather, they teach specifically to this point. They point out to the learner many examples of the applicability of what is learned in class to what occurs outside of it. It becomes even more clear now why professionals need to make a sincere effort to understand the family's dilemmas with mental illness. Unless they understand them, they cannot make the linkages between ideas presented in the classroom and what goes on at home.

The emphasis in the first part of this chapter has been on how learning takes place. The concepts of motivation, long-term retention, and learning transfer are the keys to understanding efficient and effective learning. In the next section we will present guidelines to instruction that are based on these learning concepts.

Guidelines for Instruction

Without question, the teacher is one of the important variables in the learning process. Although considerable research has been done to identify teacher characteristics that correlate with learner success, we still have little firm data regarding essential teacher characteristics. Among the few personality traits reliably correlated with effective teaching are: warmth and understanding (Ausubel, 1968); genuine interest in the subject matter and the learning process (Good & Brophy, 1977); and enthusiasm (Ryans, 1960). But these findings do not take us very far in our efforts to understand relevant teacher behaviors. As we proceed to describe the complex task of teaching and the many roles teachers play, desirable teacher qualities may become, to some degree, self-evident.

One way to describe the role of the teacher is that she or he is an instructional leader. The word "leader" may be preferred by some to "teacher," especially since the individual in question is conducting adult learning in a relatively unstructured environment. The two terms are used interchangeably here. Instructional leadership involves motivating, organizing, initiating, and guiding, as well as instructing. We are indebted to Hudgins and colleagues (1983) for a useful definition of leadership. Leadership, they state, is *entrusted* authority that is voluntarily given. *Authority* is power that is legitimate and is attached to a particular role or position. Families of the mentally ill voluntarily put their faith in the teacher, or instructional leader, who is presumed to have the knowledge and skills necessary to realize the goals of the family participants. Hudgins et al. find the following characteristics essential for successful group leadership: flexibility, assertiveness, sensitivity to others, persuasiveness, and intelligence.

Educational psychologists, including Good and Brophy (1977) and Hudgins's group, have further clarified the concept of instructional leadership by noting that its central process is decision making. Throughout a learning period, the teacher is actively and continuously engaged in making decisions. There is invariably an ongoing dynamic process underway in every learning situation; many things cannot be anticipated, so the teacher must be ready to make good judgments as to the next direction that the group should take. This gives to teaching a kind of intensity required of few other jobs. Probably a range of personality variables and behaviors figure into successful decision making, such as good preplanning, thorough knowledge of the subject matter, ability to focus on the dynamics of the group, self-confidence, and flexibility.

The overall quality of decisions in the instructional setting determines the overall quality of the educational process. Decision making is involved in every aspect of instruction: preplanning, verbal instruction, use of instructional aids, management, and support.

Preplanning

The essence of planning programs of education, simply put, is to direct attention to three basic questions: *What* do we want to accomplish? *How* can we accomplish it? *How well* did we accomplish it? Only after we become clear about what we hope to achieve can we sensibly select materials, sequence learning activities, and determine teaching strategies. If the goals of a program are too vague, instruction is apt to be inconsistent and confused, and the instructor may lose direction.

A systematic process for determining goals can be achieved through assessing the needs of the potential learners. In Chapter 4, we have discussed at some length the needs of families as assessed through various formal and informal procedures. This synthesis of findings may serve as a basis for preliminary planning of programs for families, or agencies may prefer to do their own needs assessment.

In the Maryland Family Education Program, which the author has been involved in for several years, the needs of primary focus are:

- Understanding what mental illness is.
- Knowing why patients behave as they do.
- Knowing available resources and treatments.
- Knowing appropriate expectations.
- Knowing how to motivate behavior.
- Relieving anxiety and guilt.

Once a needs assessment is made, the next step is translating those needs into educational goals. Some educational psychologists (e.g., Bedwell, Hunt, Touzel, & Wiseman, 1984) stress the importance of stating goals in terms of behavioral or performance objectives. They believe that expected outcomes should be expressed in language that stresses what the learner will be expected to do, which can then be more objectively evaluated. Some family educators may prefer to use behavioral objectives; others, like the author, may feel that they pose too many difficulties.

Good and Brophy (1977) prefer the broader terms "learning objectives" or simply "objectives." While the term "behavioral objectives" is more precise, it is more restricted in meaning and is associated with explicitly behavioristic theories and procedures. Good and Brophy favor the broader terms, since they are more inclusive of cognitive objectives. Cognitive learning, as we stated earlier, is the focus of this chapter.

Ausubel (1968) makes an even stronger case for not using behavioral objectives. Behavioral objectives, he states, give more attention to relatively trivial but readily definable goals than to goals that are intrinsically more important but resistive to precise behavioral objectives. He believes that educational psychology does not yet have the degree of sophistication and stability necessary to create a highly refined taxonomy of educational objects. We do not know enough about the underlying processes of learning and their interrelationship for precise statements of behavioral objectives to be valid. Until we do, their ability to explain these processes, as Ausubel says, is "somewhat comparable to employing a micrometer to measure inches, feet, and yards" (p. 351). In the present state of knowledge, it is more realistic and generally satisfactory to define educational objectives in grosser and more descriptive terms.

The overall purpose of the Maryland Family Education Project, for example, is to help families develop increasing competence in coping with a mentally ill person, both for the well-being of the family and for the welfare of the patient. To do so, we have given attention to three kinds of learning: cognitive learning, problem solving, and attitudinal change. Our focus here is on the cognitive learning area; the latter two objectives will be developed in the next chapter. Our general objectives for cognitive learning are:

1. To help families understand mental illness as a cognitive dysfunction due to faulty neurotransmission that becomes aggravated under conditions of stress.
2. To help families develop an empathic understanding of their relative's experience in living with severe mental illness.
3. To help families understand the current treatments for mental illness and to learn how to access available resources for care and rehabilitation.
4. To understand the nature of stress and the way it affects the vulnerable mentally ill.

These cognitive objectives, we believe, can best be achieved through verbal instruction and discussion, a description of which can be found in Chapters 5–7. This approach, as Ausubel (1968) argues, best provides for the logical arrangement and organization of ideas, thus making for better retention and more appropriate application. Random discussion does not provide the same possibilities for a useful body of knowledge.

In our experience, short lectures interspersed with discussion is most effective. Learners need a body of organized knowledge on which to base discussion, but they also need opportunities to analyze and examine ideas and relate them to what they already know. When teachers interact with learners they have the opportunity of assessing the accuracy of the learner's understanding and to note where reteaching may be necessary.

Verbal Instruction

It follows from what we learned earlier in our review of learning theory that to make verbal instruction effective, we must pay attention to the order and sequence in which ideas are organized and to the effectiveness with which these ideas are communicated.

LOGICAL ORDER

The first step in planning a lecture or verbal presentation is to review the overall objectives of the course, and, from that, to identify a more limited goal, or set of goals, that could be advanced or achieved within a learning period. The instructor must then select the most useful ideas for achieving the identified goal(s). For example, the instructor may decide that one factor that promotes effective family coping is having family members understand that neuroleptic medications play a significant role in patient stability and functioning.

To enhance the understanding of this important concept and to improve the likelihood of its long-term retention, the instructor should deliberately plan to relate the concept to the organized knowledge that the learner already possesses. Given a logical development of course material for families, material on mental illness and the role of neurotransmitter dysfunction would have already been presented. This material, then, serves as the "idea scaffolding" upon which the new instruction can be built.

Educational psychologists such as Ausubel (1968) and Hudgins et al. (1983) recommend that the ideas in a presentation be sequenced hierarchically with the more general, inclusive, and comprehensive ideas being presented first, such as that of the importance of neuroleptic medication for patient stability and functioning. Subsumed under major ideas are those of the next level of inclusiveness and generality, which might include medication's role in buffering stress and stimulation, its common side effects, its limitations, and issues of compliance surrounding it. Finally, more factual information may be supplied for each of these points, to provide clarity to the concepts. In other words, the forest is presented first and then the trees and branches. The rationale is that the more general ideas have greater explanatory power and thus provide hooks upon which more specific ideas can be hung and thus integrated and remembered.

Learning will be more effective if the instructor clearly delineates the more powerful ideas from those of lesser importance, and if the relationship between ideas is established through introductions, transitional statements, and overviews. The instructor can increase effectiveness through such perceptual organizers as schematic drawings, and underlining and outlining significant ideas. Considerable redundancy is required, but the same material should not be repeated in the same way. Rather, the imaginative teacher should plan for considerable explanation and elaboration, and should provide a variety of examples. Proper pacing means that each idea is mastered before going on to another. This recommendation may be frustrating to instructors who believe that the more facts and information crowded into an hour the better; however, merely tossing out an abundance of information does not mean an abundance of information has been learned. Quite the contrary; such an approach leads to confusion and poor retention.

COMMUNICATION SKILLS

Instructors must not only have a firm intellectual grasp of the material and its cognitive organization, but also must have the skills to communicate their ideas clearly and succinctly. In the area of mental illness, instructors must be able to translate highly technical knowledge into forms that are accurate but appropriate to the background of the family participants. Contrary to what is usually believed, it is those with the most comprehensive knowledge of a subject who can simplify it and make it comprehensible to others. Competent instructors are always vigilantly aware of signs of confusion or boredom, and are ever ready to respond to these clues with modified approaches.

Attention should be given to teaching styles that arouse and maintain interest. A lively interest, enthusiasm, and imagination are essential. Adult learners expect to be treated as equals; they are easily turned off by pompousness, dogmatism, and insincerity. Garrulousness and professional jargon should also be avoided as the first leads to confusion and boredom and the second can be offensive to those outside the profession. Families are exquisitely sensitive to the language used to describe them. Those who work with families need to know what these sensitivities are so they can avoid alienating families.

Group Interaction

Skillful leaders are sensitive to the dynamics of the groups they are leading. They deliberately work to create a climate that increases security, comfort, and involvement. They do so by keeping the total group within their span of attention at all times. Inexperienced leaders tend to overconcentrate on one or two people or get sidetracked in a long interchange with one member. Experienced leaders are also quick to pick up clues that the group is getting restless, and have the ability to tactfully reorient the discussion so that all participants are included. They are able to keep discussion on track without appearing to domineer. A generally informal style, an appreciative and friendly attitude, and a sense of humor are essential.

STIMULATING DISCUSSION

One of the more demanding tasks of instructors is to pose questions that result in lively discussion and that enhance understanding of the subject. Because this is a skill that does not come readily, some teachers consistently resort to simple questions that require simple factual answers. They often ask people to repeat information that they all had access to from a lecture or printed material. Reminiscent of our primary school days, some instructors of adults also persist in fishing for an answer from the group that lies in their heads, as though this had something to do with adult learning. This is recitation, not discussion, and is appropriate, at best, for immature learners.

When all participants have been exposed to the same background of information, it is important to determine that the material was understood and then proceed with provocative questions that lead to amplification of meaning, application of new information, or evaluation of it.

Posing questions that relate to application is recommended because this leads to a very important educational objective, transfer of learning. Families of the mentally ill have a rich store of experiential knowledge to which they can relate new information. For example, after the issue of stress management has been discussed and some general principles formulated, the instructor may ask participants to see how these principles apply in their homes—perhaps by raising some particular instances such as impending holidays. In the process of discussion, the instructor has an opportunity to assess how accurately concepts have been understood by the way they are being applied and where some reteaching may be necessary.

Questions that require evaluation can also be a stimulus to vigorous discussion. Evaluation requires placing values on things; it means making judgments of good and bad. Families are frequently having to make judgments about a vast array of issues: Is it better to have their relative living at home or in a community residence? How do they know when their expectations are too high or too low? When should they rescue their relatives and when should they let them take responsibility for their mistakes? The number of judgments that families must make are endless. If instructors pose some evaluation questions, families learn to make some of these judgments with the help of their peers.

It must be pointed out here that facts and values are not the same. One can verify facts but one cannot verify values. Having correct facts can be indispensable in making judgments, but people's beliefs and values also enter in. There is no one correct response to evaluation questions, a truth difficult for participants, or instructors for that matter, who hold their particular values as absolute.

Regardless of the kind of questions posed, a common failing of instructors is to allow participants too little time to respond. Most group leaders are familiar with the discomfort faced when a question is followed by silence. Somehow, we find it difficult to endure even a brief period of silence and if the response is not forthcoming almost immediately, we soon interrupt with meaningless remarks or by a meaningless repetition of the question. It is difficult to remember that, if a serious discussion question is posed, a period of silence must be allowed while participants are thinking and organizing their responses.

PROVIDING FEEDBACK

A final concern here is that of the instructor's feedback in response to participants' contributions. To the extent possible, ideas from the group should be related to knowledge already presented in order for the participants' organized body of knowledge to be enhanced and enriched. To do this, the instructor needs a good working knowledge of the subject matter so that she or he can spontaneously draw upon it in order to clarify and elucidate participant contributions.

Sometimes participants may make erroneous contributions to the discussion. Instructors must find tactful ways of correcting factual errors, for to leave them uncorrected may mean others in the group will accept them as true. It is important, when possible, to understand where along the way the participant may have erred. This may be learned by questioning what assumptions were made, what facts were used, and what inferences were made from observations or facts.

Instructional Materials

Instructional materials designed to help professionals develop good educational experiences for families of persons with mental illness are beginning to appear. While there are a growing number of video- and audiotapes available as well as a variety of printed materials, there has not yet been much evaluation of them, and providers are pretty much on their own in sorting out materials of the greatest usefulness and highest quality.

The guidelines for providing instruction that were developed earlier in this chapter apply equally well to the process of selecting instructional materials. Providers need to be sure that materials under consideration suit the purposes of the family educator, that they appeal to their intended audience, and that the ideas presented are clear and accurate.

The number and variety of videotapes available for family education are growing rapidly. Videotapes are an attractive medium because they heighten reality through the use of sound, color, and motion. Video presentations tend to hold interest, and they provide a common denominator of experience for group discussion. However, care should be used in their selection. Some useful guidelines are:

1. The videotape should contribute meaningfully to the subject matter under discussion. It should be the most effective tool available to achieve the purposes of the lesson. The subject matter should determine the selection of media rather than the reverse.

2. The factual material should be accurate and current. Materials in the area of mental illness must be checked carefully, since understandings in that field are undergoing rapid change.

3. The language and style of presentation should be appropriate to the families who view it, keeping in mind areas of special sensitivity to families.

Videotapes cannot be a substitute for a teacher, whose leadership is still needed. The teacher insures that the timing of the tape is appropriate and that the setting is good for viewing and discussion. Good introductions establishing a connection between what the audience already knows and the new material are essential. In addition, the teacher guides the audience in the important elements of the tape to be attended to. Meanings are further enhanced by a well-planned discussion to follow the presentation.

While videotapes are often the obvious choice for supplementary material, they are not the only possibility. Audiotapes are becoming plentiful and inexpensive. Audiotapes have a special usefulness because they can be made available for individual learning. Also, the listener can choose her or his own pace, as the material can be stopped and repeated to suit her or his particular needs.

Teachers can create their own materials, thus controlling the content to suit their instructional needs. Slides can be created without a great deal of training and with very little cost. Opaque projectors and overhead projectors are relatively inexpensive, fairly easy to operate, and provide ways for educators to display materials for classes and workshops that are specifically created to suit their purposes.

Printed materials targeted to families of the mentally ill are increasingly available. Booklets, brochures, and pamphlets are appearing everywhere. Printed material has the advantage of portability and adaptability to individual use. The rate of presentation is under the control of the reader. She or he can pace her- or himself according to individual needs, reflect on the ideas, and relate them to other relevant materials.

Summary

In this chapter, we addressed the issue of "efficiency" in learning. "Efficiency" leads to long-term retention and breadth of application of what has been learned. What matters is the clarity of presentation, the skill of organization, and the adequacy with which the material relates to existing knowledge.

The art of communication is the essence of teaching. Clarity, succinctness, and enthusiasm are much to be desired. To be avoided are verbosity, pompousness, and excessive technicality. Also to be avoided are professional jargon and portrayals of families that are perceived by them as pejorative.

CHAPTER 12

Teaching Problem-Solving Skills

It is not possible to solve every problem that families bring to classes and workshops nor would it be wise to try to do so. Effectiveness and efficiency dictate that we teach families to solve their own problems independently. We create a basis for effective problem solving when we build a strong foundation of knowledge about mental illness, but knowledge alone is not a guarantee of effective problem solving.

"A problem occurs," write Hudgins et al. (1983), "when the individual is confronted with a situation for which he has no solution" (p. 343). As we have reiterated many times, families of the mentally ill face a great array of problems—some seemingly small but persistent and frustrating and others of nearly overwhelming proportions. Like most people trying to solve problems, families are likely to use trial and error solutions, with many random tries until success emerges. This approach is inefficient and time consuming. We believe that more formalized problem-solving approaches will result in more efficient solutions.

Falloon, Boyd, and McGill (1984) have made significant contributions to our thinking regarding ways to teach families problem-solving techniques. The problem-solving skills that families of the mentally ill use are probably not significantly different from those used by many other families. Their problem-solving strategies may well have been adequate for most situations, but they may not be adequate for the special problems posed by mental illness. Even so, as Falloon et al. acknowledge, some families arrive independently at very effective techniques.

The issue of whether, and to what extent, problem-solving skills are trainable has had a long and confused history, and the tendency has been to ignore the issue. It is an important issue, however, for a central part of many educational and psychoeducational programs across the country is skills training in problem solving. Ausubel (1968) notes that the most widespread approach to training in problem solving is to instruct the learner in various general principles garnered from theoretical analysis and from comparing the strategies of successful and unsuccessful problem solvers. These general principles are:

1. Formulate and delimit the problem.
2. Explore many possible solutions.
3. Evaluate the alternatives and select the best solution.
4. Implement the solution.
5. Evaluate the outcome; re-plan if needed.

We appreciate the fact that these are very general principles applicable to a wide range of problems. Their applicability to problems that families face with mental illness may not be readily apparent. Family education teachers face a special challenge in demonstrating how these general principles can help families solve day-to-day problems.

Defining the Problem

Sometimes families participating in a workshop or class have difficulty identifying many troubling problems. Although they express general discontent, discouragement, and frustration, they find it hard to say why. They may have tolerated so many pressures for so long that they have become inured to it all, or they may feel that with such a devastating disease as a mental illness, reasonable satisfaction in living is not to be expected. Kanter (1985) suggests that families ask themselves the following questions: Do you really have control over your home and family affairs? Are your possessions safe? Do you have personal privacy? Does your relative have personal habits that threaten the safety and well-being of others? Does your relative treat you with respect and consideration? These are battles that, given energy and persistence, can be won. He cautions families against starting with the most difficult and consequential problems such as getting a job or becoming independent. He reasons that dealing with one's immediate environment in an orderly and respectful manner is a prerequisite to handling more complex tasks.

Families' first attempts to identify problems are likely to result in such broad problem statements as: "He manages money poorly";

"She doesn't take care of her health"; "He doesn't cooperate"; or "He is too messy." Although varying in their degree of generality, they are all too general to generate specific plans of attack. It takes time to delimit the problem to a specific behavior that will lend itself to a precise solution. Families need to be guided in precise definitions and to be cautioned against taking on more than one problem at a time. If they have many areas of concern, they might first choose the one, not that causes them the most distress, but that they have a reasonable chance of being successful with.

Let us take some examples. The Wilson family is totally exasperated because their son, Jerry, handles money poorly. They relate that no matter how much money he receives, he soon returns and says he is broke. When Mr. Wilson asks him what happened to his money, he says, "There wasn't enough." The Wilsons need a solution to this dilemma. But first they must decide what precisely *is* the problem? It may be delimited in one of several ways:

> Jerry really does not have enough money to cover basic expenses.
> Jerry does not know how to budget.
> Jerry knows his family will supplement, so he does not try to budget.
> Large amounts of Jerry's money cannot be accounted for.

Before they can go further in solving the problem, the Wilsons need to agree on the most accurate definition of the problem. In this case, the Wilson family, taking into consideration all aspects of the problem, decided that Jerry did not know how to stick to a budget. They are now ready to take the next step, that of exploring possible solutions. Before going to Step 2, let us take one more example of problem formulation.

The Anderson family is most concerned about their daughter's messiness. They have been reminding Laura endlessly about the importance of being neat and how irritating her messiness is to others, and have even threatened to make her move out. Their pleas fall on deaf ears. Obviously, messiness is too general a problem; hence, the family will need to decide which of her messy behaviors bothers them most. The more specific problems they might come up with are:

> Wet towels and water are left on the floor after Laura's showers.
> Laura leaves food out and kitchen counters messy after snacks.

Laura's room is strewn with clothes, make-up, records, and bedding.

The living room is cluttered with Laura's coats and sweaters, books, and ashtrays.

The family agrees that these are all annoying problems but decides that the bathroom has been the source of the most complaints. Their next step is to explore the various ways that they might accomplish a needed change in this area. We will now give attention to this exploratory stage.

Generating Alternative Solutions

Once family members have reached a consensus on defining the problem, the next step is to generate a list of possible solutions. The idea is to develop several suggestions before making a decision about the best one. The leader of a family education group acknowledges all suggestions without making judgments about their plausibility and tactfully discourages families from making premature choices. Full consideration must be given to all proposed situations.

One might question the reason for this fairly time-consuming process. Research on problem solving has shown that the first idea that occurs in a response to a question is likely to be the least original and imaginative and that the time and effort spent in generating new ideas pays off. It compels the problem solver to avoid narrow attention to a fixed aspect of the problem and to go beyond the obvious. Good problem solvers stay flexible and suspend judgment until all possible solutions are weighed. This takes time. Impatient family educators must keep in mind that it is the process that is important. Once families learn the process, presumably they can apply it to a variety of problems that arise.

We will illustrate this process of generating solutions by returning to the case of the Wilson family, who defined its problem as: How can we help Jerry budget his money? Some of the various solutions that might be discussed are:

- Give Jerry daily allowances rather than weekly ones.
- Have Jerry keep track of his expenditures for a week to see where his money goes.
- Shop with Jerry.
- Refuse to give him extra money when his allowance is gone.

- Sit down with Jerry and develop a budget plan.
- Threaten to send him back to the hospital.
- Get him a budget book.

The next and most difficult step will be to weigh these alternatives and select the best one.

The Anderson family will go through a similar process of generating solutions. They have defined their problem as: How can we get Laura to clean up the bathroom after she has showered? Some things they might do are:

- Show her specific steps in doing the job.
- Embarrass her in front of her grandparents about her sloppiness.
- Not allow her to the breakfast table until the work has been done.
- Agree to do half the cleanup in exchange for her doing the other half.
- Give her extra cigarettes when she complies.

The list might go on, but we have illustrated our point. The next step is to review these alternatives and come up with a solution.

Evaluating Alternatives and Selecting the Best Solution

In order to facilitate the process, a quick screening of alternative solutions might be done to eliminate those least plausible. Three to five alternatives are probably all that can profitably be examined and compared at a given time. It is important that families realize that there are no perfect solutions. Each solution invariably has both positive and negative consequences. Sometimes the most optimal solution is a combination of a number of alternatives. The main considerations, of course, are the likelihood that the plan will solve the problem identified and that the solution will have the least negative consequences for all those involved in the situation.

The first consideration, then, is: Will the chosen plan work? This is a question difficult for families to predetermine. Of course, no complete certainty can be given. Families must draw on their understanding of their relative and what has and has not worked before. They may have to re-plan strategies several times before success is reached.

People with mental illnesses frustrate and baffle their families because they often do not respond to explanations and reasoning. Thus, families need to assess the different pressures that can be brought to bear to achieve compliance with requests. Essentially, we are talking about what leverage families have available to them to enhance the likelihood of change in behavior. The following options might be considered:

1. *Use strategies that preclude the unacceptable behavior from occurring.* Examples of this kind of an approach include the following: Put a lock on the telephone if it is being used to make an excessive number of expensive calls; take away house keys if there are too many unwelcome visits; lock the bedroom door if personal privacy and possessions are not being respected. Sometimes these approaches can be a quick and certain means of solving a problem with a minimum of hassle. Their limitations are, however, that these kinds of solutions are not possible for all problems, and where they are possible, they merely prevent negative behavior. They do not teach how to use a telephone properly, nor how to relate to others respectfully. Nevertheless, where the stakes are high in safety, lost money, and aggravation and the patient will not respond readily to other means, a little imagination may result in finding a way to eliminate the possibility of the troublesome behavior occurring.

2. *Eliminate any family behaviors that reinforce undesirable patient behaviors.* With a little examination, families sometimes discover that they are unintentionally rewarding patient behaviors that they do not like. If exploitative behavior, argumentativeness, or physical threats wear families down or frighten them, they probably give in to demands for a little peace of mind. It is soon clear to these families that their relative knows that these tactics work and that she or he will continue using them. There is really only one solution, which is not to let such tactics get the person what she or he wants. This sounds easy but it may not be. Some patients can become very obnoxious and even threatening. A carefully planned strategy may need to be developed in which the family thinks through what patient responses are likely, and then develops plans to deal with these behaviors.

If the family decides not to reward careless handling of records by not giving more money, they may have to be prepared to ignore whining and arguing. They may need to be aware of ways their relative gets to their vulnerable spots by accusing them of "caring only about money"; "not wanting them to have any pleasure"; or "being selfish and middle class." By anticipating these kinds of attacks, families can school themselves not to respond. Probably any response they make will lead to an argument. They should simply say, "I don't want to discuss it further" and walk away from the situation.

3. *Let the patient suffer the consequences of her or his behaviors.* Some misbehaviors eventually bring on their own undesirable consequences. Suffering the consequences of one's behaviors can be a powerful way to learn, and it leaves little room to blame others. For most misbehaviors it is worth asking: Will this misbehavior eventually bring its own negative consequences? The difficult part for families, then, is to avoid intervening and rescuing the person from the consequences of her or his actions. The person who squanders her or his cigarette rations may have to do without; the one who fails to check her or his tires may have to walk a few miles back to town; and the one who constantly loses keys will have to do her or his own tedious search. Each of these leads to a little discomfort that may motivate the person to better behavior. But families have difficulty just standing by and letting their relative struggle. They are so aware that their relative suffers a lot because of mental illness, and would gladly intervene to prevent any more discomfort. Some may worry that even these minor stressors could lead to a setback for the patient.

We are not advocating that mentally ill people always suffer the consequences of their actions. There are some consequences that can be deleterious to them. Prolonged exposure to weather, lack of food and needed health care, and vulnerability to personal attack are some obvious examples. The consequences for failing to go to the dentist can be dental disease and extractions, which the person may learn from, but we would consider this consequence too severe. Not only may the consequence be too damaging to the mentally ill person, but the cost may be too high for the family. Sometimes families must intervene to avoid costly losses to property, high legal fees, or a complete dissolution of a system of community care that had been painstakingly put together for the patient.

4. *Create positive or negative consequences.* Most families have control over some resources or some privileges that they can use as leverage to control their relative's behavior. If the mentally ill relative expresses desires for something—a record, dinner out,

some new clothes, use of the car, or whatever—the family can then negotiate some change in behavior in exchange for granting the patient's wish. While this approach might seem to some families as tiresome and ungenerous, it may be the only way to shape undesirable behavior.

Some families may say that they have no leverage, but if they are asked to list all that they do for their relative to make her or him comfortable and happy, they become aware of the various resources over which they have control. Again, families may be reluctant to add to their relative's discomfort by withholding something, and they may even fear retribution.

We will now return to the cases of the two families that we have been using in this chapter to illustrate problem solving. The Wilson family's problem was how to get their son, Jerry, to stick to a weekly budget. They generated seven possible alternative solutions, and after weighing the pros and cons of each, they decided to combine two alternatives. The plan became to sit down with Jerry and help him develop a weekly budget plan, and to refuse to give him extra money when the weekly allowance was gone. The Anderson family, working on a bathroom problem with their daughter, quickly dismissed a couple of alternatives and agreed on one solution: Laura would not be allowed at the breakfast table until the bathroom passed inspection after her use.

While arriving at a plan of action is hard enough, implementing the plan is even more demanding. At this point in the process, families should be guided in anticipating the likely chain of events once the patient is informed of the decision, and if or when negative consequences are applied. Families should expect that their requirements will be tested and that more than likely they will have to apply predetermined sanctions. Families must decide at this point if they are comfortable taking these actions. If they anticipate that they are likely to give in if their relative reacts badly, then it is much better not to start at all.

Implementing the Plan

The patient is entitled to a clear, concise statement as to what is expected of her or him, including any positive or negative consequences that apply. It is not enough to say that the bathroom must be cleaned up. Patients must be told that towels must be hung up, water wiped up from the floor, toiletries put back in their designated places, and so forth. The time for this to be completed should be stated. These directions should be given in a firm, calm, noncontentious manner, reflecting confidence that this decision is correct and that requests will be met.

Families sometimes report that when they try to direct their relative a long argument ensues and before long they are off on another topic that is not germane to the problem. They conclude that trying to do something about their relative's problem is such a hassle that it is not worth it. We suggest that the only discussion that is relevant to this point relates to the patient's understanding of what is expected of her or him. Families must prepare themselves to refuse to respond to anything else. They should also avoid becoming defensive about their decision. Some patients are masters at detecting their relative's vulnerable spots and know precisely how to get them on the defensive. In this way, families can be successfully diverted from following through on their plan.

One important reason for defining the desired behavior precisely is that it facilitates one's ability to decide if expectations have been met. The judgment must be made as to whether the patient has met the expected behavior to the best of her or his ability or not. Then families must follow through with whatever consequences were promised.

Evaluating the Plan

The final step of problem solving is to review the results. Solving problems is an ongoing process and is rarely fully successful with one effort. Considerable re-planning may be required.

Generalizing Problem-Solving Skills

Helping families solving one or more problems does not insure that they will be able to solve subsequent problems independently. We cannot assume that skills generalization will occur without specifically working toward that. Much of what we have said about transferring knowledge in the last chapter applies to transferring problem-solving skills from one situation to another. The key in both cases lies in the way we establish a relationship between the specific and the general. It is general principles of problem solving and broad general concepts that transfer to new situations. For this to occur, the learner must have many experiences in the application of the general to the specific in a variety of situations.

Summary

Families face a host of difficult problems as they cope with their mentally ill relative day-by-day. A program that merely provides answers to these problems is not efficient and effective over the long run unless families understand how to generalize beyond the immediate situation. We recommend that families learn generic problem-solving skills that enhance the possibility that they will be able to solve most problems independently.

CHAPTER 13

Providing Emotional Support to Families

In an earlier chapter, we have described the pain and emotional turmoil that families experience when they learn of their relative's mental illness. They live under catastrophic levels of stress as they try to cope with the disturbed individual, come to terms with their own grief and disappointment, and learn the vagaries of the mental health system. We have stressed the importance of teaching families about the illness and providing them with practical problem-solving skills. Attention to the effectiveness of teaching, however, is not enough. Families need considerable emotional support to see them through the turmoil that will dominate their lives.

Sarason (1985) urges clinicians to become aware of the effect that one person's illness or handicap can have on the lives of the rest of the family. He quotes extensively from the book *Parents Speak Out* by Turnbull and Turnbull (1978), in which families of retarded children talk about the generally callous treatment that they have received from professionals. The parents who speak out in this book happen to be professionals who themselves have mentally retarded children, but who were no less intimidated by the system nor felt any better understood than any other parent. This leads Sarason to wonder about "the psychological and financial price we pay for professional behavior that neither repairs, dilutes, nor prevents personal misery" (p. 101). Essentially all the complaints that families of the retarded child made have also been reported by families with mentally ill members.

Clearly more attention must be given to the quality of family support that is given when these tragedies occur. Attention must be given to the concept "support," what it means to be supportive, and common barriers to effective support. The word "support" occurs frequently in popular and professional vocabularies and is assumed to be a good thing. But support is rarely defined, and people use the term in a variety of ways. The professional community has provided little understanding of the concept, and there is a significant lack of research indicating how support works in strengthening people's coping capacities.

The Concept of Support

We have drawn primarily from the field of psychotherapy for whatever it could offer to our understanding of supportive relationships. Winston, Pinsker, and McCullough (1986) recently presented a synthesis of what has been written about supportive therapy. They concluded that too little has been written about supportive treatments probably because too many professionals see supportive therapy as being inferior to that of insight therapy. Some of these professionals seem to believe that supportive therapy patronizes and infantilizes, thus undermining self-confidence and self-esteem. They believe it is a simpleminded approach and easily practiced. Winston et al. do not agree with these contentions and neither do we. We feel that the capacity to provide support is essential when working with people living under high levels of stress.

The aim of supportive psychotherapy, according to Winston and colleagues, is to increase the person's adaptive capacities and to help her or him reaffiliate with others. It is not the same as insight therapy; for instance, it is primarily interested in the here and now rather than in the relationship of the past to the present. Supportive aspects of treatment, they say, are noncognitive and are not primarily aimed at understanding. Rather, they are meant to convey to people their value, and that their feelings and predicaments are being accurately understood. The authors draw from Hollis (1964) to provide some of the various aspects of supportive therapy:

1. Sustaining procedures. The therapist demonstrates interest, desire to help, and understanding to the client. She or he expresses confidence in the client's abilities or competence, and provides reassurance with regard to the anxieties that the client is experiencing.

2. Procedures of direct influence. In supportive treatment, the clinician uses suggestion and advice to help the person deal with immediate stressors in her or his life.

3. Catharsis or ventilation. The clinician must be a good listener, who encourages the stressed individual to freely express her or his anxiety, pain, disappointment, and grief. This kind of ventilation is part of the healing process.

4. Reflective consideration of the current situation, alternative courses, and the use of available resources.

We find Hollis's suggestions pertinent with regard to developing the concept and method of providing support to families with mentally ill relatives. Contributions to our thinking have come from other sources as well. Bernheim (1982), for example, was one of the first to use the term "supportive counseling" in relation to families of the mentally ill. She stressed the importance of support by noting that family interventions that ignore this need have a certain predictable outcome: They increase the family's level of anxiety, guilt, depression, anger, and frustration, and they lower the level of adaptive responses. The goals of supportive counseling, according to Bernheim, are not only to secure the family's cooperation, but also to repair its members' self-esteem, and relieve feelings of helplessness.

Often families are led to believe that the purpose of help to families is solely to help the patient. They expect little understanding for the practical problems they face and even less for the emotional turmoil they experience. While it is important for the family to feel that it has done the best that it can for the patient, even to the point of having made substantial sacrifice, families who fail to invest energy and time in other members will find their resources quickly sapped. Such families need to be encouraged to take better care of themselves, and to make use of whatever community facilities exist to relieve their burden (Bernheim, 1982).

Bernheim makes the observation that for most providers, training has not prepared them to take on this supportive role. She says, "We are prepared to view the family as being responsible for the patient's problem. We are prepared to view independence from one's family of origin as the right and proper goal of treatment. We are not prepared to divulge to the patient or to the family little of what we know—and of what we do not know" (1982, p. 640).

In his recent book, Sarason (1985) examines with considerable concern professional's lack of capacity for what he calls "caring and compassion." He believes that the world view into which mental health trainees are initiated renders them insensitive to the phenomenological plight of the individual they are supposed to be helping. As we noted earlier in this book, theories as they are currently taught do not include the ideas of being caring and compassionate. The growth of self-help groups, Sarason argues, is evidence of the dissatisfaction that many people feel about the caring community. People in these groups feel that only those who have the condition can understand it.

Sarason points out that the qualities of caring and compassion have not been studied and that there is very little training in understanding the nature and expression of caring and compassion. Sarason feels that there has been too much emphasis on objectivity and too much worry about "emotional involvement." He cites as additional barriers our large bureaucratic institutions, the way we select students for admission into mental health training institutions, and our overemphasis on training in technical skills.

Sarason stresses that compassion and caring involve pain, inconvenience, and self-sacrifice. They also require a large measure of maturity and self-understanding. Sarason makes the cogent statement that understanding does not come full-blown but rather as a result of grappling with three major obstacles: underestimating the scope and complexity of the problem; failure to use one's life experiences creatively; and resistance to the idea that the process is unending.

It is our contention that the foundation for supportive relationships lies in empathy and acceptance, which will be discussed next.

Empathy

Rogers (1961) states that an accurate and empathic understanding of the client's world as seen from the inside is necessary in order to be helpful and avoid alienating the client. We must ask ourselves, Rogers says, "Can I let myself enter fully into the world of his feelings and personal meanings and see these as he does: Can I step into his private world so completely that I lose all desire to evaluate and judge it?" (p. 53). One is being empathic when what the client is thinking and feeling is understandable to the extent that if one were in the client's place one would feel the same way as she or he does.

Caring and compassion, Sarason (1985) says, require the professional to understand other people in their complexity, to become them even if they are widely different in values, style, actions, and purpose. Sarason cautions us to remember that the clinician's world is not that of the troubled individual, and the clinician must exercise control over the tendency to project the values of her or his own world. He reminds us, further, that compassion and caring require an unusual degree of self-understanding, so that one can see commonalities between self and others.

Probably most professionals want to be empathic with people and, indeed, most probably believe that they are. However, intent is not enough—the clinician's actions must be experienced as compassionate. The clinician must use language and behavior that communicates empathic feelings. In this regard, the work of Havens (1978), in which he explored the uses of language in validating another's experience, is instructive. Havens reminds us that empathic understanding can be communicated through the use of short, felt utterances by which the other's feeling state is acknowledged. Such utterances as "Oh dear," "How awful," or "Really?" are examples of empathic language when they are accompanied by the appropriate tone of voice and facial expression. Sometimes no words need be spoken; just tone and gesture can convey the meaning. Of most importance is to attend to the reaction of the other person. If that person appears to be encouraged to share more of her or his foremost feelings and deepen her or his narrative flow, the helper can assume that an accurate understanding of the other's situation has been conveyed. If the person stops or changes the subject, the clinician must assume that she or he has failed to communicate an accurate perception of what is being shared.

At issue here is what to tell mental health professionals who want to develop and communicate more empathic understanding to families. Sarason (1985) advises us to analyze the reasons why compassion and caring are in such short supply. From such an analysis, each of us might find something personally applicable. Sarason feels that we have not been taught to go beyond the presenting problem to include the phenomenological plight of the individual, nor do we understand the consequences of one person's suffering for her or his family. For some time we have urged changes in professional training, so that students are exposed extensively to families and learn about the family dilemmas firsthand. Since few practitioners have received this kind of training, those who expect to be educators of families must conscientiously seek to fill in the gap themselves. Chapter 2 of this book provides a good introduction to the topic, but it is only a beginning and as we learned from a statement of Sarason quoted earlier in this chapter, we should not underestimate the complexity of the other person's world, nor should we ignore the fact that growth in capacity for empathy is a continuous process that is never complete.

Sarason (1985) feels that mental health professionals mean well but have a "parochialism" that robs them of the opportunity to be compassionate. The elderly, parents, mentally ill people, blacks, and those with different life styles have frequently criticized clinicians for their lack of empathic understanding. Educators of families can overcome their parochialism by drawing from their own experiences with tragedy and catastrophe, whether or not they were ones of mental illness. As we noted in Chapter 2, the literature on stress and coping has shown that there are real commonalities of experience among people coping with a great variety of disasters in their lives. By the time that most people have finished their training, it is likely that they have experienced some painful, and perhaps tragic, events that can make them more empathic to others. Using their own experiences creatively and continuing to expose themselves to new revelations of the family experience can help them to overcome parochialism.

Schneider (1985), in his foreword to Sarason's book, turns our attention again to the problem of professional training. He says that compassion and caring are thought to violate the first tenet of clinical relationships—"Thou shalt not muddy the boundaries between clinician and client" (p. xiv). He believes that professionals are socialized in ways that enhance feelings of distance and superiority. Family educators need to make significant efforts to overcome the degree of objectification of others that has been a part of their training.

Schneider cites as another problem the tendency to overemphasize the importance of technical applications to people's problems to the neglect of understanding them. We have stated elsewhere (Hatfield & Lefley, 1987) that we believe that much of the present alienation of families is due to the excessive emphasis on technique and the lack of emphasis on empathic understanding. While we have given significant attention to the techniques of instruction in this volume, we still insist that understanding is of foremost importance. Family educators are urged to focus on understanding families first and only secondarily on instructional technique.

Acceptance

When families are fully accepted by the helping professional, they become less defensive and more adaptive. The word "acceptance" gets bandied around a lot, so we need to define what we mean.

Rogers (1961) has given us a concept of acceptance that can serve us well. He says that acceptance means having a warm regard for the other person as a person of unconditional self-worth—of value no matter what her or his condition, feelings, or behavior. The clinician must respect the patient as a separate person, entitled to possess her or his own feelings in her or his own way. It means an acceptance of and regard for her or his attitudes of the moment, no matter how negative or positive, no matter how much they contradict other attitudes held in the past. Genuine acceptance is antithetical to judgmentalism and labeling.

Frank (1973) believes that the professional helper must genuinely care about the welfare of the person being helped. This does not necessarily mean approval, he says, but rather a determination to persist, to care enough to make a genuine investment in the person.

Both Frank and Rogers emphasize the importance of genuineness in helping relationships. Rogers advises us to avoid playing a role or assuming a facade. To do this, one must get in touch with one's own feelings. With regard to families of the mentally ill, Anderson, Reiss, and Hogarty (1986) caution against using artificial praise or rapid reassurance. They feel that this leaves the family feeling misunderstood or cut off prematurely. They urge clinicians to be optimistic, but at the same time anchored firmly in reality.

If empathy, warmth, acceptance, and genuineness are to be communicated to families in an educational setting, then care must be given as to how that class is conducted. Clearly, it must be small and informal with a lot of interaction between the instructor and participants. In our experience, a class of 12 to 15 is the maximum number desirable. An accepting and understanding atmosphere is necessary so that families can feel nondefensive and free to share their own pain, discouragement, and anxiety. Usually, it is best if the same leader remains throughout all the sessions so that there is ample time for her or him to get to know the participants. Instruction is provided in small increments with ample time in between so that participants can discuss what they learned and relate it to their own situations.

Much of the support in a class or workshop can come from other family members. The skilled leader encourages interaction between participants by identifying members who have had experiences that relate to the problems of others. The leader need not be the authority on everything that comes before the group. Some family members have a large accumulation of experience that can be valuable to others in the group. Hence, interaction should be encouraged.

Families have great capacity for empathizing with one another. There is great comfort in talking to somebody who is or has been in your shoes. Leaders have an excellent opportunity to promote such support in classes and to link up their participants with the local affiliates of the National Alliance for the Mentally Ill (NAMI) for ongoing support. It is now generally believed that social support plays a major role in modifying or mitigating the deleterious effects of stress on health.

Peer Support to Families

Of key importance in determining the outcome of a crisis is the absence or availability of social supports in the environment. People depend on one another for affirmation. Since classes for families are necessarily time-limited, it is important that families find a supportive network outside of the group or that the group continue on its own as a source of social support. Caplan (1974) defines a social support system as attachments between individuals and groups of individuals that promote mastery of emotions, offer guidance, provide feedback, validate identity, and foster competence.

Social networks are particularly important during times of major life changes. The onset of mental illness in the family is certainly a time of major life changes. For many families NAMI has become the family's new community in that it provides them with a new identity and the needed social support.

For those unfamiliar with NAMI, some understanding of it is needed in order that linkages can be established between unaffiliated families and the organization. NAMI was organized in 1979 in the wake of a self-help trend that had been rapidly emerging since World War II. A large number of these groups tended to form around conditions that lack a medical cure, and in which there is a residue of impairment, as well as remaining problematic medical, social, and psychological effects. The practice of medicine is now based in an older model appropriate for acute illnesses; doctors do not always understand the frustrations of adaptation to a chronic disability. Self-help groups spring up to supply the missing support and education that is needed (Hatfield, 1987b).

The definition of self-help groups supplied by Katz and Bender (1976) will help providers understand the self-help and support activities of NAMI. Self-help groups are

> voluntary small group structures for mutual aid in the accomplishment of a specific purpose. They are usually formed by peers who have come together for mutual assistance in satisfying a common need, overcoming a common handicap or life-disrupting problem, and bringing about desired social and/or personal change. The initiators and members of such groups perceive that their needs are not or cannot be met by or through existing social institutions. (p. 9)

The emergence of self-help organizations has led to new ways to solve difficult problems of living. What is unique is that they focus on peer support and education and rely less heavily on professionals and agencies.

Gartner and Riessman (1977, p. 7) state that the following list of features are critical to self-help groups and serve to distinguish them from other voluntary groups.

1. Self-help groups always involve face-to-face interactions.
2. The origin of self-help groups is usually spontaneous (not set up by some outside group).
3. Personal participation is an extremely important ingredient.
4. The members agree on and engage in some actions.
5. Typically the groups start from a condition of powerlessness.
6. The groups fill needs for a reference group, a point of connection and identification with others, a base for activity, and a source of ego reinforcement.

There is considerable agreement among social scientists as to the ways in which self-help groups benefit their members (Katz, 1961; Killilea, 1982; Tracy & Gussow, 1976):

1. Members serve as role models to each other. Members note how other people cope with a particular dilemma and begin modeling their own behavior after them.

2. Help giving is reciprocal and inherently therapeutic. Knowledge gained from personal experience is highly valued. People who have been recipients of help can give help in return, making them feel less powerless and more useful. They feel interpersonally competent when they are fulfilling the obligations and expectations of mutual support.

3. Opportunities for learning are provided. There are few other educational opportunities that are as appropriate to the situation as those found in self-help organizations. Outsiders who do not live with the situation on a daily basis do not always understand. Learning from peers means getting information in an understandable form.

There may be considerable differences in style between informal systems such as self-help groups and the more formal approaches of professionals. There are strengths in each of them. Collaboration between the two systems is possible if there is an understanding of the strengths and weaknesses of each.

Summary

It is our belief that a predominantly educational approach to families does not preclude providing a good measure of support to them. However, if we are serious about providing support, we must give significant attention to the kinds of attitudes and behaviors that are conducive to support and the barriers in ourselves and in our institutions that mitigate against families feeling supported. Central to the concept of support is empathy or the ability to enter the inner world of another. If we empathize with families who have mentally ill relatives, we understand the personal meaning that mental illness has for them, we share their pain and frustration, and we communicate to them that we understand how hard it is and how much the family does for the sake of their ill relative. When we are truly empathic, it is impossible to be judgmental.

Issues in Program Development

It is not our intention with this book to produce a model of a family education program that can be replicated in various agencies and institutions across the country. We believe that attempts to clone model programs and transfer them to different settings have not been generally successful in the mental health field. What we have attempted to do is to provide basic information about mental illness and some basic principles of instructional technique, with the expectation that creative providers can then develop programs uniquely appropriate to their own situations. Since agencies and institutions differ significantly across the country and the people that they serve have their own unique characteristics, programs must be tailor-made for each situation. This chapter provides a summary of some of the issues that professionals should consider as they contemplate creating family education programs.

Some General Issues

Bernheim and Switalski (1988) have pointed out in a recent article that the desire to provide educational workshops and classes for families is becoming quite commonplace. This has not always been true. As we indicated earlier, educational approaches have recently been offered as a more suitable alternative than family therapy to help families cope with mental illness in a member. Much enthusiasm has been expressed for the new approaches with concomitant scorn for the "dark ages" of family therapy. But some dogmatism is beginning to appear about the best ways to do family education or psychoeducation that should be avoided. Present states of knowledge do not warrant great certainty as to the best way to work with families.

Practitioners who are thinking about setting up a program for families will necessarily have to consider three issues: the nature of the agency in which they are working; the characteristics of families in their geographical area; and their own educational and leadership qualifications. These factors preclude the adoption of ready-made programs.

Characteristics of the Situation

Most practitioners who are considering offering a program to families will be attached to an agency or institution that deals with mental illness. Some may be working out of an advocacy organization such as the Mental Health Association (MHA) or the National Alliance for the Mentally Ill (NAMI). Still others may work directly under state or local mental health administrations. The Maryland Family Education Program, which will be discussed later, is an example of the latter structure. Still others may be a part of an adult education program in a high school or a college. These situational factors can be influential in the effectiveness of a program.

It is difficult to launch a new program unless the leadership of an agency and a fair majority of its staff understand what you are trying to do and are philosophically compatible with it. If most of the staff have an orientation to families that is substantially different, it is unlikely that a successful program can be begun. It may be necessary to delay beginning a program until the staff can be exposed to current educational approaches through workshops, lectures, and printed material.

Resistances to starting educational programs are not unusual, but it is often difficult to identify the real reasons for the opposition. There certainly can be legitimate philosophical differences about the best ways to work with families. These ought to be subject to open discussion and an examination of relevant literature. It is important not to belittle the approaches that others favor and not to create a defensiveness that will be difficult to overcome. Resistances to change can come from many sources. It is to be expected that many professionals will feel threatened by new ways of doing things. They may have considerable investment in their present therapies, feel like experts at what they are doing, and feel reluctant to substitute new approaches in which they see themselves as novices. These are understandable behaviors and must be dealt with sensitively.

Bernheim and Switalski (1988) stress the importance of trying to get everyone in an agency to involve themselves in issues concerning families. They point out that considerable difficulty may arise if isolated, piecemeal efforts are made at involving families. Families often come into contact with a range of people in an agency, each of whom has a different area of expertise. What is more, each may have a substantially different attitude toward patients and toward the role that they feel families should play. The institution or agency as a whole must be prepared to support a collaborative relationship with the families.

Some providers strongly committed to family programs have been keenly disappointed in the failure of their efforts to entice families into the programs that they have created. Families simply do not show up. While sometimes this might be due to negative attitudes that families associate with the particular agency, there may be other reasons that have to do with the characteristics of the families who were invited.

Characteristics of the Families

It is too much to expect that all families will find a particular program suited to their needs and their learning styles. Families vary tremendously. When we offer something to families, we tend to feel that everyone "ought" to attend. But it is not for us to say what is good for everyone. Only the families themselves can know what suits their purposes. Some of the variations in populations that should be considered when planning a class or workshop are:

1. *Economic and educational backgrounds.* Some families may have transportation problems, difficulty getting off of work, or excessive fatigue due to working two jobs. They may be taking care of elderly relatives, or they may have poor health themselves. Some may have literacy problems or limited education, making it difficult for them to understand technical information. We have obligations to these families as well as to those easier to approach. This means tailoring the information for them. It may also involve creating materials with low-reading demand and using films and video, and it may mean taking education to families in their homes.

It is our experience that some providers tend to underestimate the life complexities that many families face. They feel critical of those families that are not willing to undergo great inconvenience or hardship in order to attend their programs. There is a tendency to write off these families as "dysfunctional," "multiproblemed," or "not caring." Such conclusions are defeatist. If the programs offered do not fit the families' needs, there should be a continued effort to create ones that do.

2. *Relationships to the patient.* Programs that now exist for families tend to address those who are parents of young adult chronic patients. Hence, materials and programs that address the needs of spouses, siblings, and adult children of mentally ill parents need to be developed.

3. *Length of experience with mental illness.* The needs of families going through a first episode of mental illness may differ significantly from those of families who have been coping with the illness for many years. The first group of families may need a great deal of support, and their primary concerns may be for survival skills that will help see them through those devastating early episodes. Veteran families may be thinking more about long-term problems such as how to help their relative make a transition from dependence on the home to dependence on peers and the community; how to balance the needs of all family members; and how to prepare their relative for the time when the parents are no longer alive.

These are just a few of the ways that providers should look at the populations that they wish to serve. Undoubtedly, there are many other considerations such as the ethnic makeup of potential participants, the current locality of the patient, how much direct caregiving the family gives. Obviously, there is much more that needs to be addressed.

Leader Characteristics

Success in family education rests significantly on the qualities of leaders or teachers. While there is no "right" kind of personality for this kind of work, there are attitudes and abilities that can make a significant difference. Luckily most of them can be learned. Frequently mentioned in this book is the necessity for the leaders to be nonjudgmental and nonblaming in their relationships with families. Most families are hypersensitive about the way they are viewed by professionals and are certain to pick up on negative attitudes. Leaders must have an understanding about how difficult it is to live with a mentally ill person and not offer their suggestions as though they were a panacea. It is easy to give advice, but trying to carry it out is another matter.

Leaders need to be well prepared, with an understanding of mental illness, current treatments, the needs of families, and practical coping strategies. In addition, they need to have a general understanding of the process of learning, how to organize materials for effective learning, and how to teach for broad application. Leaders also need to be skilled in group processes and able to maintain the involvement of all members in the group.

In terms of methodology, leaders need to be able to weigh carefully various instructional techniques that might be used and to consider their appropriateness for various kinds of individuals. Role playing might be suitable for some, but turn others off. Some groups may be willing to share a great deal of personal experience with mental illness; others may be reluctant. Homework may be welcomed by some, but be rejected by others. There is no evidence to show that any one of these techniques has advantages over any other. Leaders must feel comfortable and competent in using them, and they must be quick to assess their participants' comfort when these techniques are introduced. It is important to focus first and foremost on the participants and not to get overly zealous about a particular technique.

Some leaders of current educational programs feel that it is essential to have peer co-leaders in each group. This can be very helpful at times, but it may not always make a difference. If a peer-leader is chosen as a co-leader, she or he should not be a token leader, but should fully share responsibility for the class. Some inexperienced leaders may welcome a family co-leader to give them feedback about the usefulness of the material they are presenting and to reflect back to them how they are being perceived by families. Other leaders may prefer to rely on their own perceptions and to collect adequate evaluative material from participants.

The Maryland Family Education Program

The Maryland Family Education Program began evolving about 8 years ago and is still evolving. It began as a response to the needs identified by families in the Maryland affiliates of NAMI. A large percentage of Maryland families were directly caring for patients and finding the demands often beyond their coping capacities. The available family therapies were costly and not available to everyone, and many families reported that they were degrading and not suited to their needs. The Program was started by the author, then a professor of education at the University of Maryland, with a grant from the Office of Human Resources Development of the Mental Hygiene Administration of the Maryland Department of Health and Mental Hygiene. The Program has now taken on several aspects of training for families and for professionals interested in learning more about working with families.

Unique to this program is its base in a state mental health administration with the program leader and two part-time assistants traveling to agencies and institutions across the state to provide services when requested. Agencies make their own determination of the need for this service and serve as host to whatever event is planned.

The nucleus of the program consists of 4 to 6 weeks of evening classes for families based on the knowledge and philosophy exemplified in this book. Each class has a co-leader from the host agency who serves as an apprentice to the visiting leader in order to develop the necessary skills to lead classes independently. The basic curriculum of the class is contained in a booklet written for families called *Coping with Mental Illness in the Family: A Family Guide* (Hatfield, 1989a), with instructional assistance available in a companion booklet, *Coping with Mental Illness in the Family: A Leader's Guide* (Hatfield, 1989b).

Workshops on family education are now available all over the state to providers who want an introduction to such topics as: understanding mental illness; understanding families of the mentally ill; and effective leadership and instruction. Also, several conferences are developed each year to enhance the knowledge and skills of family educators. An advisory committee of family educators across the state help plan these events and keep the program leader informed with regard to provider needs.

This is an evolving program, hence, there must be considerable program adaptation to meet many of the needs that have been identified but not yet addressed. Foremost at this time is the need to create appropriate kinds of help to low-income families who do not ordinarily come to classes or workshops. An experiment in outreach to these families is under way, in which education will be taken to their homes.

In Conclusion

The new directions in working with families of the mentally ill tend to be educational in approach. There is considerable enthusiasm for the new programs now being developed and much stated or implied criticism of the old ones. In the eyes of some, the right approach to families has finally arrived and those who do not go along with it are considered rigid and unbending. It is important to remember at this point that historically all programs in mental health started out as new and fresh approaches to difficult problems. But new programs soon become old and a new generation of practitioners become scathing in their denunciation of outmoded methods and ideas. Perhaps, we can avoid having these newer educational approaches become rigid and unchanging in the future, as well as objects of rejection and scorn.

We need to learn how to keep new ways of doing things continually changing and evolving. Gardner's (1965) small book on renewal and innovation is instructive in this regard. Gardner identifies a wide range of obstacles to renewal, most of which occur in people's minds rather than in external arrangements. New ideas soon become established ways of doing things when people begin thinking all pioneering has been done, all the exciting things already tried. Little by little, preoccupation with method, technique, and procedure gains subtle dominance over the whole process. Means triumph over ends. In other words, there is increasing emphasis on the right way to do things.

Gardner further points out that problems of vested interest soon creep into new programs. Research dollars, status, and reputation are accumulations that weigh one down and bind one to the status quo. Gardner advises us to learn to "travel light" and to maintain a tentative relationship with our ideas and our commitments. An organization may avoid experimental ventures because it fears to risk its reputation for soundness. Many a gifted innovator has allowed her or his creative talent to be smothered by a growing commitment to her or his own previously stated doctrine. Many an established specialist fears the loss of reputation if she or he ventures beyond the territory where she or he has proved her or his mastery. In many organizations, established ways of doing things are continued not by reason of logic nor even by habit but by the force of one powerful consideration: Changing them would jeopardize the rights, privileges, and advantages of many people.

The answer to continuous innovation lies within individuals. No one knows for certain why some individuals stagnate and others continue to evolve and grow. Self-renewing individuals, Gardner believes, avidly pursue the exploration of their own potential to the end of their days. They possess considerable self-knowledge and courageously face their own emotions, anxieties, and fantasies. They can tolerate considerable ambiguity in their experience, and they are able to live with uncertainty and suspended judgment.

This book represents our best effort to conceptualize new directions in work with families of the mentally ill. It is not a finished idea, because we believe no such ideas can ever be finished. It is up to the next generation of creative individuals to pick up where we have left off and to evolve these ideas in still newer directions.

REFERENCES

Adler, P. (1982). An analysis of the concept of competence in individual and social systems. *Community Mental Health Journal, 18,* 34–39.

Alvarez, W. C. (1961). *Minds that came back.* New York: Lippincott.

Anderson, C. M., Reiss, D. J., & Hogarty, G. E. (1986). *Schizophrenia and the family: A practitioner's guide to psychoeducation and management.* New York: Guilford Press.

Andreasen, N. (1984). *The broken brain: The biological revolution in psychiatry.* New York: Harper & Row.

Anonymous. (1955). An autobiography of a schizophrenic experience. *Journal of Abnormal and Social Psychology, 51,* 677–687.

Anscombe, R. (1987). The disorder of consciousness in schizophrenia. *Schizophrenia Bulletin, 13,* 241–260.

Anthony, W. A., & Liberman, R. P. (1987). The practice of psychiatric rehabilitation: Historical, conceptual, and research base. *Schizophrenia Bulletin, 12,* 542–559.

Antonovsky, A. (1979). *Health, stress, and coping.* San Francisco: Jossey-Bass.

Appley, M. H., & Trumbull, R. (1977). On the concept of psychological stress. In A. Monat & R. S. Lazarus (Eds.), *Stress and coping: An anthology.* New York: Columbia University Press.

Ausubel, D. (1968). *Educational psychology: A cognitive view.* New York: Holt, Rinehart & Winston.

Bateson, G., Jackson, D., Haley, J., & Weakland, J. (1956). Toward a theory of schizophrenia. *Behavioral Science, 1,* 251–264.

Bedwell, L., Hunt, G., Touzel, T., & Wiseman, D. (1984). *Effective teaching: Preparation and implementation.* Springfield, IL: Charles C. Thomas.

Beels, C. C. (1978). Social networks, the family, and the schizophrenic patient. *Schizophrenia Bulletin, 4,* 512–520.

Beels, C. C., & McFarlane, W. R. (1982). Family treatments of schizophrenia: Background and state of the art. *Hospital & Community Psychiatry, 33,* 541–549.

Bernheim, K. (1982). Supportive family counseling. *Schizophrenia Bulletin, 8,* 634–640.

Bernheim, K., & Lehman, A. (1985). *Working with families of the mentally ill.* New York: Norton.

Bernheim, K. F., & Lewine, R. R. (1979). *Schizophrenia: Symptoms, causes, treatments.* New York: Norton.

Bernheim, K., Lewine, R. R., & Beale, C. T. (1982). *The caring family.* New York: Random House.

Bernheim, K., & Switalski, T. (1988). The Buffalo family support project. *Hospital & Community Psychiatry, 39,* 663–665.

Bigge, M., & Hunt, M. (1962). *Psychological foundations of education.* New York: Harper & Row.

Bowen, M. (1960). A family concept of schizophrenia. In D. D. Jackson (Ed.), *The etiology of schizophrenia.* New York: Basic Books.

Brown, C. W., Birley, J. L. T., & Wing, J. K. (1972). Influence of family life on the course of schizophrenic disorders: A replication. *British Journal of Psychiatry, 121,* 241–258.

Brundage, B. E. (1983). First person account: What I wanted to know but was afraid to ask. *Schizophrenia Bulletin, 9,* 585–586.

Bruner, J., & Connolly, K. (1974). Competence: Its nature and nurture. In K. Connolly & J. Bruner (Eds.), *The growth of competence.* New York: Academic Press.

Bugen, L. A. (1980). Human grief: A model of prediction and intervention. In P. W. Powers & A. E. Dell Orto (Eds.), *Role of the family in rehabilitation of the physically disabled.* Baltimore: University Park Press.

Burton, A. (1974). The alchemy of schizophrenia. In A. Burton, J. Lopez-Ibor, & W. Mendel (Eds.), *Schizophrenia as a life style.* New York: Springer.

Caplan, G. (1970). *The theory and practice of mental health consultation.* New York: Basic Books.

Caplan, G. (1974). *Support systems and community mental health.* New York: Behavioral Publications.

Carpenter, W. T. (1986). Thoughts on the treatment of schizophrenia. *Schizophrenia Bulletin, 12,* 527–539.

Clausen, J., & Yarrow, M. R. (1955). The impact of mental illness on the family. *Journal of Social Issues, 11*(4), 3–24.

Coelho, G. W., Hamburg, D. A., & Adams, J. E. (Eds.). (1974). *Coping and adaptation.* New York: Basic Books.

Cournos, F. (1987). The impact of environmental factors on outcome in residential programs. *Hospital & Community Psychiatry, 38,* 848–851.

Cross, K. P. (1981). *Adults as learners.* San Francisco: Jossey-Bass.

Dauner, M. (1986). The future of payment for psychiatric illness. In J. Talbott (Ed.), *Our patients' future in a changing world.* Washington, DC: American Psychiatric Press.

Davis, G. C., & Akiskal, H. S. (1986). Descriptive, biological, and theoretical aspects of borderline personality disorder. *Hospital & Community Psychiatry, 37,* 685–692.

Dewar, T. R. (1978). The professionalization of the client. *Social Policy, 8,* 4–9.

Diamond, R. J. (1984). Increasing medication compliance in young adult chronic psychiatric patients. In B. Pepper & H. Ryglewicz (Eds.), *Advances in treating the young adult chronic patient* (New Directions for Mental Health Services, No. 21). San Francisco: Jossey-Bass.

Dincin, J. (1975). Psychiatric rehabilitation. *Schizophrenia Bulletin, Summer,* 131–147.

Ellis, H. (1965). *The transfer of learning.* New York: Macmillan.

Falloon, I. R. H., Boyd, J. L., & McGill, C. W. (1984). *Family care of schizophrenia: A problem-solving approach to the treatment of mental illness.* New York: Guilford Press.

Feldman, D. J. (1980). Chronic disabling illness: A holistic view. In P. W. Powers & A. E. Dell Orto (Eds.), *Role of the family in rehabilitation of the physically disabled.* Baltimore: University Park Press.

Figley, C. R., & McCubbin, H. I. (Eds.). (1983). *Stress and the family: Coping with catastrophe* (Vol. II). New York: Brunner/Mazel.

Fish, G. (1985, September). What it's like to be chronically depressed. *Indiana Community Support System Network News,* Indiana Department of Mental Health.

Fleming, R. C. (1981). Cognition and social work practice: Some implications of attribution and concept attainment theories. In A. N. Mallucio (Ed.), *Promoting competence in clients.* New York: Free Press.

Flynn, L. (1987). The stigma of mental illness. In A. B. Hatfield (Ed.), *Families of the mentally ill: Meeting the challenges* (New Directions for Mental Health Services, No. 34). San Francisco: Jossey-Bass.

Ford, M. E. (1985). The concept of competence: Themes and variations. In H. A. Marlowe & R. B. Weinberg (Eds.), *Competence development.* Springfield, IL: Charles C. Thomas.

Frank, J. (1973). *Persuasion and healing: A comparative study of psychotherapy* (rev. ed.). Baltimore: Johns Hopkins University Press.

Frank, R., & Kamlett, M. (1985). Direct costs and expenditures for mental health care in the United States in 1980. *Hospital & Community Psychiatry, 36,* 165–167.

Franks, D. (1987). *The high cost of caring: Economic contributions of families to the care of the mentally ill.* Unpublished dissertation, Brandeis University.

Freedman, M. A. (1974). Subjective experience of perceptual and cognitive disturbances in schizophrenia. *Archives of General Psychiatry, 30,* 333–340.

Fromm-Reichmann, F. (1948). Notes on the development treatment of schizophrenia by psychoanalytic therapy. *Psychiatry, 11,* 263–273.

Gardner, J. W. (1965). *Self renewal: The individual and the innovative society.* New York: Harper & Row.

Gartner, A., & Riessman, F. (1977). *Self-help in the human services.* San Francisco: Jossey-Bass.

Gaylin, S. (1985). The coming of the corporation and the marketing of psychiatry. *Hospital & Community Psychiatry, 36,* 154–159.

Godschalx, S. M. (1985). The challenge of chronicity. In D. L. Crichley & J. T. Maurin (Eds.), *The clinical specialist in psychiatric mental health nursing: Theory, research, and practice.* New York: Wiley.

Godschalx, S. M. (1986). *Experiences and coping strategies of people with schizophrenia.* Unpublished doctoral dissertation, University of Utah.

Goldman, H. H. (1982). Mental illness and family burden. *Hospital & Community Psychiatry, 33,* 557–560.

Goldschmidt, W. (1974). Ethology, ecology, and ethnological realities. In G. W. Coelho, D. A. Hamburg, & J. E. Adams (Eds.), *Coping and adaptation.* New York: Basic Books.

Goldstein, M. J. (1981). *New developments in interventions with families of schizophrenics.* San Francisco: Jossey-Bass.

Good, T., & Brophy, J. (1977). *Educational psychology: A realistic approach.* New York: Holt, Rinehart & Winston.

Gottlieb, B. (1976). Lay influence on the utilization and provision of health services: A review. *Canadian Psychological Review, 17,* 126–136.

Greist, J. H., & Jefferson, J. W. (1984). *Depression and its treatment.* Washington, DC: American Psychiatric Press.

Guerney, B., Stollak, G., & Guerney, L. (1971). The practicing psychologist as educator—an alternative to the medical practitioner model. *Professional Psychology, 3,* 276–282.

Gunderson, J. G. (1984). *Borderline personality disorder.* Washington, DC: American Psychiatric Press.

Haley, J. (1980). *Leaving home: The therapy of disturbed young people.* New York: McGraw-Hill.

Hansell, H. (1976). *The person-in-distress: On the biosocial dynamics of adaptation.* New York: Human Sciences Press.

Hanson, S. M. H., & Sporakowski, M. J. (1986). Single parent families. *Human Relations, 35,* 3–8.

Harding, C. M., Zubin, J., & Strauss, J. S. (1987). Chronicity in schizophrenia: Fact, partial fact, or artifact. *Hospital & Community Psychiatry, 38,* 477–485.

Harris, M., & Bergman, H. (1984). The young adult chronic patient: Affective responses to treatment. In B. Pepper & H. Ryglewicz (Eds.), *Advances in treating the young adult chronic patient* (New Directions for Mental Health Services, No. 21). San Francisco: Jossey-Bass.

Hatfield, A. (1978). Psychological costs of schizophrenia to the family. *Social Work, 23,* 355–359.

Hatfield, A. (1979). The family as partner in the treatment of mental illness. *Hospital & Community Psychiatry, 30,* 338–340.

Hatfield, A. (1983). What families want of family therapists. In W. R. McFarlane (Ed.), *Family therapy in schizophrenia.* New York: Guilford Press.

Hatfield, A. (1984). The family consumer movement: A new force in service delivery. In B. Pepper & H. Ryglewicz (Eds.), *Advances in treating the young adult chronic patient* (New Directions for Mental Health Services, No. 21). San Francisco: Jossey-Bass.

Hatfield, A. (1985). *A consumer guide to mental health services.* Arlington, VA: National Alliance for the Mentally Ill.

Hatfield, A. (1986). Semantic barriers to family and professional collaboration. *Schizophrenia Bulletin, 12*(3), 325–333.

Hatfield, A. (1987a). Coping and adaptation: A conceptual framework for understanding families. In A. B. Hatfield & H. P. Lefley (Eds.), *Families of the mentally ill: Coping and adaptation.* New York: Guilford Press.

Hatfield, A. (1987b). Social support and family coping. In A. B. Hatfield & H. P. Lefley (Eds.), *Families of the mentally ill: Coping and adaptation.* New York: Guilford Press.

Hatfield, A. (1987c). Systems resistance to effective family coping. In A. Myerson (Ed.), *Barriers to treating the chronic mentally ill* (New Directions for Mental Health Services, No. 33). San Francisco: Jossey-Bass.

Hatfield, A. (1989a). *Coping with mental illness in the family: A family guide* (2nd ed.). Arlington, VA: National Alliance for the Mentally Ill.

Hatfield, A. (1989b). *Coping with mental illness in the family: A leader's guide.* Arlington, VA: National Alliance for the Mentally Ill.

Hatfield, A., Farrell, E., & Starr, S. (1984). The family's perspective on homelessness. In H. R. Lamb (Ed.), *The homeless mentally ill.* Washington, DC: American Psychiatric Press.

Hatfield, A., Fierstein, R., & Johnson, D. M. (1982). Meeting the needs of families of the psychiatrically disabled. *Psychosocial Rehabilitation Journal, 6,* 27–40.

Hatfield, A. B., & Lefley, H. P. (Eds.). (1987). *Families of the mentally ill: Coping and adaptation.* New York: Guilford Press.

Havens, L. (1978). Exploration in the uses of language in psychotherapy: Simple empathic statements. *Psychiatry, 41,* 336–345.

Hersch, C. (1972). Social history, mental health, and community control. *American Psychologist, 27,* 749–753.

Hill, R. (1986). Life cycle stages for types of single parent families: Of family development theory. *Family Relations, 35,* 19–30.

Hirsch, S., & Leff, J. (1975). *Abnormalities in parents of schizophrenics.* London: Oxford University Press.

Hirschowitz, R. G. (1976). Groups to help people cope with the tasks of transition. In R. G. Hirschowitz & B. Levy (Eds.), *The changing mental health scene.* New York: Spectrum.

Hoenig, J., & Hamilton, M. W. (1966). The schizophrenic patient in the community and his effect on the household. *International Journal of Social Psychiatry, 12,* 165–176.

Hogarty, G. E., Anderson, C. M., Reiss, D. J., Kornbleth, S. J., Greenwald, D. P., Javna, C. D., & Madonia, M. J. (1986). Family psychoeducation, social skills training, and maintenance chemotherapy in the after-care treatment of schizophrenia. *Archives of General Psychiatry, 43,* 633–641.

Holden, D. F., & Lewine, R. R. (1982). How families evaluate mental health professionals. *Schizophrenia Bulletin, 8,* 628–633.

Hollander, R. (1980). A new service ideology: The third mental health revolution. *Professional Psychology, 11,* 561–566.

Hollis, F. (1964). *Casework: A psychosocial therapy.* New York: Random House.

Holmes, T. H., & Rahe, R. H. (1967). The social readjustment rating scale. *Journal of Psychosomatic Research, 11,* 213–218.

Howe, J. (1985). A family perspective on the APA report: The homeless mentally ill. *Psychosocial Rehabilitation Journal, 8,* 15–20.

Howell, M. (1973). *Helping ourselves: Families and the human network.* Boston: Beacon Press.

Howells, J. G., & Guirguis, W. R. (1985). *The family and schizophrenia.* New York: International Universities Press.

Hudgins, B., Phye, G., Schau, C., Theisen, J., Ames, C., & Ames, R. (1983). *Educational psychology.* Itasca, IL: Peacock.

Intagliata, J., Willer, B., & Egri, G. (1986). Role of the family in case management of the mentally ill. *Schizophrenia Bulletin, 12,* 699–708.

Janis, I. L. (1974). Vigilance and decision making in personal crises. In G. V. Coelho, D. A. Hamburg, & J. E. Adams (Eds.), *Coping and adaptation.* New York: Basic Books.

Jefferson, L. (1964). I am crazy wild this minute. How can I learn to think straight? In B. Kaplan (Ed.), *The inner world of mental illness.* New York: Harper & Row.

Johnson, D. (1984). The needs of the chronically mentally ill: As seen by the consumer. In M. Mirabi (Ed.), *The chronically mentally ill: Research and services.* New York: Spectrum.

Johnson, D. (1987). Professional–family collaboration. In A. Hatfield (Ed.), *Families of the mentally ill: Meeting the challenges* (New Directions for Mental Health Services, No. 34). San Francisco: Jossey-Bass.

Judd, L. (1986). The future of the basic science of psychiatry. In J. A. Talbott (Ed.), *Our patients' future in a changing world.* Washington, DC: American Psychiatric Press.

Kanter, J. S. (1984). *Coping strategies for relatives of the mentally ill.* Arlington, VA: National Alliance for the Mentally Ill.

Kanter, J. S. (Ed.). (1985). *Clinical issues in treating the chronic mentally ill* (New Directions for Mental Health Services, No. 27). San Francisco: Jossey-Bass.

Kaplan, B. (1964). *The inner world of mental illness.* New York: Harper & Row.

Katz, A. H. (1961). *Parents of the handicapped—Self-organized parents' and relatives' groups for the treatment of ill and handicapped children.* Springfield, IL: Charles C. Thomas.

Katz, A. H., & Bender, E. I. (1976). *The strength in us: Self-help groups in the modern world.* New York: New Viewpoints.

Kazak, A. E., & Marvin, R. S. (1984). Differences, difficulties, and adaptation: Stress and social networks in families with a handicapped child. *Family Relations, 33,* 67–78.

Killilea, M. (1982). Interaction of crisis theory, coping strategies, and social support systems. In H. C. Schulberg & M. Killilea (Eds.), *The modern practice of community mental health.* San Francisco: Jossey-Bass.

King, C. (1987). Dissolving the barriers: Reflections on coming out of the closet. *Hang Tough,* Marin Network of Mental Health Clients, San Anselmo, CA.

Klein, J. (1983). The least restrictive alternative: More about less. *Psychiatric Quarterly, 55,* 106–114.

Kline, N. S. (1974). *From sad to glad.* New York: Ballantine Books.

Knowles, M. (1984). *The adult learner: A neglected species* (3rd ed.). Houston: Gulf Publishing Co.

Krauss, J. B., & Slavinsky, A. T. (1982). *The chronically ill psychiatric patient in the community.* Boston: Blackwell.

Lamb, H. R. (1982). *Treating the long-term mentally ill.* San Francisco: Jossey-Bass.

Lamb, H. R., & Oliphant, E. (1978). Schizophrenia through the eyes of the family. *Hospital & Community Psychiatry, 29,* 803–805.

Landis, C., & Mettler, F. A. (1964). *Varieties of psychopathological experience.* New York: Holt, Rinehart & Winston.

Lazarus, R. (1977). The nature of coping. In A. Monat & R. Lazarus (Eds.), *Stress and coping: An anthology.* New York: Columbia University Press.

Leete, E. (1987). A patient's perspective on schizophrenia. In A. B. Hatfield (Ed.), *Families of the mentally ill: Meeting the challenges* (New Directions for Mental Health Services, No. 34). San Francisco: Jossey-Bass.

Leff, J., & Vaughn, C. (1985). *Expressed emotion in families.* New York: Guilford Press.

Lefley, H. P. (1987a). Behavioral manifestations of mental illness. In A. B. Hatfield & H. P. Lefley (Eds.), *Families of the mentally ill: Coping and adaptation.* New York: Guilford Press.

Lefley, H. P. (1987b). Culture and mental illness: The family role. In A. B. Hatfield & H. P. Lefley (Eds.), *Families of the mentally ill: Coping and adaptation.* New York: Guilford Press.

Lefley, H. P. (1987c). The family's response to mental illness in a relative. In A. B. Hatfield (Ed.), *Families of the mentally ill: Meeting the challenges* (New Directions for Mental Health Services, No. 34). San Francisco: Jossey-Bass.

Levine, M. (1981). *The history and politics of community mental health.* New York: Oxford University Press.

Lickey, M. E., & Gordon, B. (1983). *Drugs for mental illness.* New York: Freeman.

Lidz, T. (1973). *The origin and treatment of schizophrenic disorders.* New York: Basic Books.

MacDonald, N. (1960). The other side: Living with schizophrenia. *Canadian Medical Association Journal, 82,* 218–221.

MacKinnon, B. L. (1977). Psychotic depression and the need for personal significance. *American Journal of Psychiatry, 134,* 427–429.

Madanes, C. (1981). *Strategic family therapy.* San Francisco: Jossey-Bass.

Maluccio, A. N. (1981). Competence-oriented social work practice: An ecological approach. In A. N. Maluccio (Ed.), *Promoting competence in clients: A new/old approach to social work practice.* New York: Free Press.

Marrone, J., Horgan, J., Scripture, D., & Grossman, M. (1984). Serving the severely psychiatrically disabled client within the VR system. *Psychosocial Rehabilitation Journal, 8*(2), 5–23.

Maxmen, J. S. (1985). *The new psychiatry.* New York: Morrow.

May, P. R. A. (1968). *Treatment of schizophrenia: A comparative study of five treatment methods.* New York: Science House.

McCubbin, H. I., & Patterson, J. M. (1983). Family transitions: Adaptation to stress. In H. I. McCubbin & C. R. Figley (Eds.), *Coping with normative transitions* (Vol. I). New York: Brunner/Mazel.

McElroy, E. M. (1987). The beat of a different drummer. In A. B. Hatfield & H. P. Lefley (Eds.), *Families of the mentally ill: Coping and adaptation.* New York: Guilford Press.

McFarlane, W. R. (Ed.). (1983). *Family therapy in schizophrenia.* New York: Guilford Press.

McGhie, A., & Chapman, J. (1961). Disorders of attention and perception in early schizophrenia. *British Journal of Medical Psychology, 34,* 103–116.

McGrath, M. E. (1984). First person account: Where did I go? *Schizophrenia Bulletin, 10,* 638–640.

McGuire, T. G. (1981). *Financing psychotherapy—costs, effects, and public policy.* Cambridge, MA: Ballenger.

McKnight, J. (1977). The professional service business. *Social Policy, 8,* 110–116.

Mechanic, D. (1974). Social structure and personal adaptation: Some neglected dimensions. In G. V. Coelho, D. A. Hamburg, & J. E. Adams (Eds.), *Coping and adaptation.* New York: Basic Books.

Mechanic, D. (1978). Considerations in the design of mental health benefits under national health insurance. *American Journal of Public Health, 68,* 482–488.

Mechanic, D. (1980). *Mental health and social policy.* Englewood Cliffs, NJ: Prentice-Hall.

Meenaghan, T., & Mascari, M. (1971). Consumer choice, consumer control in service delivery. *Social Work, 16*(4), 50–57.

Mendel, W. M. (1974). The phenomenological theory of schizophrenia. In

J. J. Lopez-Ibor, A. Burton, & W. M. Mendel (Eds.), *Schizophrenia as a life style*. New York: Springer.

Minkoff, K. (1978). A map of the chronic mental patient. In J. Talbott (Ed.), *The chronic mental patient*. Washington, DC: American Psychiatric Press.

Minkoff, K., & Stern, R. (1985). Paradoxes faced by residents being trained in the psychosocial treatment of people with chronic schizophrenia. *Hospital & Community Psychiatry, 36,* 859–864.

Monat, A., & Lazarus, R. (Eds.). (1977). *Stress and coping: An anthology*. New York: Columbia University Press.

Moos, R. H. (Ed.). (1976). *Human adaptation: Coping with life crises*. Lexington, MA: Heath.

Newman, B. M., & Newman, P. R. (1975). *Development through life*. Homewood, IL: Dorsey Press.

Papolos, D. F., & Papolos, J. (1987). *Overcoming depression*. New York: Harper & Row.

Parad, H. (Ed.). (1965). *Crisis intervention: Selected readings*. New York: Family Services Association of America.

Park, C. C., & Shapiro, L. N. (1976). *You are not alone: Understanding and dealing with mental illness*. Boston: Little, Brown.

Pasamanick, B., Scarpetti, F., & Dinitz, S. (1967). *Schizophrenia in the community*. New York: Appleton-Century-Crofts.

Peretz, D. (1970). Development, object-relationships, and loss. In B. Schoenberg, A. Carr, D. Peretz, & A. Kutscher (Eds.), *Loss and grief: Psychological management in medical practice*. New York: Columbia University Press.

Rabkin, J. (1984). Community attitude and local facilities. In J. Talbott (Ed.), *The chronic mental patient: Five years later*. New York: Grune & Stratton.

Rapoport, L. (1965). The state of crisis: Some theoretical considerations. In H. J. Parad (Ed.), *Crisis intervention: Selected readings*. New York: Family Services Association of America.

Rogers, C. (1961). *On becoming a person*. Boston: Houghton-Mifflin.

Ryans, D. G. (1960). *Characteristics of teachers*. Washington, DC: American Council on Education.

Sabshin, M. (1986). The future of psychiatry: Coping with "new realities." In J. A. Talbott (Ed.), *Our patients' future in a changing world*. Washington, DC: American Psychiatric Press.

Sarason, S. B. (1981). *Psychology misdirected*. New York: Free Press.

Sarason, S. B. (1985). *Caring and compassion in clinical practice*. San Francisco: Jossey-Bass.

Schell, R. E., & Hall, E. (1979). *Developmental psychology today* (3rd ed.). New York: Random House.

Schneider, S. (1985). Foreword. In S. Sarason (Ed.), *Caring and compassion in clinical practice*. San Francisco: Jossey-Bass.

Schopler, E., & Mesibov, G. B. (1984). Professional attitudes toward parents: A forty-year progress report. In E. Schopler & G. B. Mesibov (Eds.), *The effects of autism on the family.* New York: Plenum Press.

Schopler, E., Mesibov, G. B., Shigley, R., & Bashford, A. (1984). Helping autistic children through their parents: The TEACCH model. In E. Schopler & G. B. Mesibov (Eds.), *The effects of autism on the family.* New York: Plenum Press.

Sechehaye, M. (1964). Excerpts from autobiography of a schizophrenic girl. In B. Kaplan (Ed.), *The inner world of mental illness.* New York: Harper & Row.

Sechehaye, M. (1970). *Autobiography of a schizophrenic girl.* New York: New American Library.

Segal, S. P., Everett-Dille, L., & Moyles, E. W. (1979). Congruent perceptions in the evaluation of community-care facilities. *Journal of Community Psychology, 7,* 60–68.

Selye, H. (1956). *The stress of life.* New York: McGraw-Hill.

Sharfstein, S., & Beigel, A. (1985). Introduction. In S. Sharfstein & A. Beigel (Eds.), *The new economics and psychiatric care.* Washington, DC: American Psychiatric Press.

Sharp, M. L. (1987). Schizophrenia—how it feels. *Newsletter of the Alliance for the Mentally Ill of Tucson and Southern Arizona, 4,* 1.

Shore, D. (1986). *Schizophrenia: Questions and answers.* Rockville, MD: National Institute of Mental Health.

Snyder, K. (1984). Education for families of schizophrenic patients: Rationale, annotated review, and users guide. In M. Goldstein, L. Casolino, & K. Snyder (Eds.), *Education for families with schizophrenic members.* Rockville, MD: Office of Prevention, National Institute of Mental Health.

Stearns, A. (1984). *Living through personal crisis.* Chicago: Thomas More Press.

Steinman, R., & Traunstein, D. (1986). Redefining deviance: The self-help challenge to human services. *Journal of Applied Behavioral Science, 16,* 347–368.

Strauss, J. S. (1986). Discussion: What does rehabilitation accomplish? *Schizophrenia Bulletin, 12,* 720–723.

Swan, R. W., & Lavitt, M. R. (1986). *Patterns of adjustment to violence in families of the mentally ill.* New Orleans: Elizabeth Wisna Research Center, Tulane University School of Social Work.

Talbott, J., & Dauner, M. (1985). An insurance executive looks at changing patterns of health care. *Hospital & Community Psychiatry, 36,* 160–164.

Terkelsen, K. G. (1987a). *Educational approaches to working with families of the mentally ill.* A conference sponsored by the National Alliance for the Mentally Ill, Arlington, VA.

Terkelsen, K. G. (1987b). The meaning of mental illness to the family. In

A. B. Hatfield & H. P. Lefley (Eds.), *Families of the mentally ill: Coping and adaptation.* New York: Guilford Press.

Torrey, E. F. (1983). *Surviving schizophrenia: A family manual.* New York: Harper & Row.

Torrey, E. F., & Wolfe, S. M. (1986). *The care of the seriously mentally ill: A rating of state programs.* Washington, DC: Public Citizen Research Group.

Tough, A. (1979). *The adult's learning projects.* Toronto: Ontario Institute for Studies in Education.

Tracy, G. S., & Gussow, Z. (1976). Self-help groups: A grass-roots response to needs for services. *Journal of Applied Behavioral Science, 12,* 310–316.

Turnbull, A. P., & Turnbull, H. R. (1978). *Parents speak out.* Columbus, OH: Merrill.

Vine, P. (1982). *Families in pain: Children, siblings, spouses, and parents speak out.* Westminster, MD: Pantheon.

Walsh, M. (1985). *Schizophrenia: Straight talk for families and friends.* New York: Morrow.

Warren, F. (1984). The role of the National Society in working with families. In E. Schopler & G. B. Mesibov (Eds.), *The effects of autism on the family.* New York: Plenum Press.

Wasow, M. (1982). *Coping with schizophrenia: A survival manual.* Palo Alto, CA: Science & Behavior.

Wechsler, J., Wechsler, N., & Karpf, H. (1972). *In a darkness.* New York: Norton.

White, R. (1974). Strategies of adaptation: An attempt at systematic description. In G. V. Coelho, D. A. Hamburg, & J. E. Adams (Eds.), *Coping and adaptation.* New York: Basic Books.

White, R. W. (1976). Strategies of adaptation. In R. H. Moos (Ed.), *Human adaptation: Coping with life crises.* Lexington, MA: Heath.

Wikler, L., Wasow, M., & Hatfield, E. (1981). Chronic sorrow revisited: Parents vs. professional depiction of the adjustment of parents of mentally retarded children. *American Journal of Orthopsychiatry, 51,* 63–70.

Winston, A., Pinsker, H., & McCullough, L. (1986). A review of supportive therapy. *Hospital & Community Psychiatry, 37,* 1105–1114.

Wrubel, J., Benner, P., & Lazarus, R. S. (1981). Social competence from the perspective of stress and coping. In J. D. Wine & M. D. Smye (Eds.), *Social competence.* New York: Guilford Press.

Wynne, L. C. (1987). Family relations and communications: concluding comments. In L. C. Wynne, R. M. Cromwell, & S. Matthysse (Eds.), *The nature of schizophrenia.* New York: Wiley.

Wynne, L., McDaniel, S., & Weber, T. (1987). Professional politics and the concepts of family therapy, family consultation, and systems consultation. *Family Process, 26,* 153–166.

Zelt, D. (1981). First person account: The Messiah quest. *Schizophrenia Bulletin, 7,* 527–531.